Student Workbook

by
Robert H. Marshall
Donald H. Jacobs
Allen B. Rosskopf
Charles J. LaRue

AGS Publishing
Circle Pines, MN 55014-1796
800-328-2560

MW00995163

© 2004 AGS Publishing
4201 Woodland Road
Circle Pines, MN 55014-1796
800-328-2560 * www.agsnet.com

AGS Publishing is a trademark and trade name of American Guidance Service, Inc.

Printed in the United States of America

ISBN 0-7854-3648-0

Product Number 93963

A 0 9 8 7 6 5 4 3 2

Table of Contents

Unit 2

Unit 3

Unit 4

Unit 1

Systems of Measurement

Directions The table describes some units of measurement. Each unit has a metric equivalent. Complete the table with the help of a dictionary or other reference tool. The first item is done for you.

Units of Measurement

Unit	Description	Equals (Metric)
1. knot	unit used to measure air and wind speed	about 1.9 kilometers per hour
2. carat	unit of weight for gemstones	
3. hand	unit of length for measuring height of horses	
4. league	unit of distance in measuring land: about 3 miles	
5. light-year	unit of distance equal to the distance light travels through space in one year	
6. furlong	unit of distance in measuring land: 220 yards	
7. pound	unit of weight	
8. fathom	unit of length used to measure the depth of water	
9. cable	unit of length used at sea, equal to 120 fathoms	
10. gallon	unit of liquid volume	
11. span	unit of length, based on the spread of fingers	
12. rod	unit of length for measuring land	
13. ell	unit for measuring cloth	
14. peck	unit of volume used to measure grains and fruit	
15. foot	unit of length	

Adding and Subtracting Metric Units of Length

Directions Add or subtract the numbers in each problem. Then simplify your answer. Write your answer on the line. The first one is done for you.

1.   12 centimeters 5 millimeters
   +   5 centimeters 3 millimeters   17 centimeters 8 millimeters _____

2.   10 meters 8 centimeters
   +   9 meters 9 centimeters   _____

3.   22 meters 4 centimeters
   +   3 meters 5 centimeters   _____

4.   20 meters 10 millimeters
   +   23 millimeters   _____

5.   10 centimeters 5 millimeters
   + 22 centimeters 8 millimeters   _____

6.   6 meters 2 centimeters
   +   4 meters   _____

7.   23 millimeters
   +   3 millimeters   _____

8.   11 meters 9 millimeters
   +   8 meters 6 millimeters   _____

9.   39 meters 9 millimeters
   −   1 meter 6 millimeters   _____

10.   20 meters 7 centimeters
   −   5 centimeters   _____

Using Metric Units to Find Area

Directions Use the formula to find the area of each figure.
Write your answer on the line. Include the unit in your answer.

area = length × width

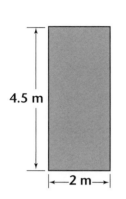

4.5 m

2 m

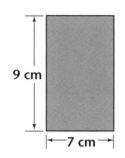

9 cm

7 cm

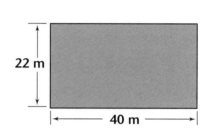

22 m

40 m

1. _____

2. _____

3. _____

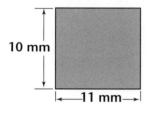

10 mm

11 mm

2.5 cm

6.5 cm

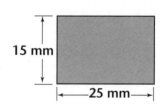

15 mm

25 mm

4. _____

5. _____

6. _____

Directions Write the missing number on the line. Be sure to include the unit in the answer.

7. $6 \text{ m} \times$ _____ $= 48 \text{ m}^2$

8. $12 \text{ cm} \times 18 \text{ cm} =$ _____

9. $14 \text{ mm} \times$ _____ $= 1{,}400 \text{ mm}^2$

10. $120 \text{ m} \times 17 \text{ m} =$ _____

11. $8.5 \text{ mm} \times 3.5 \text{ mm} =$ _____

12. $35 \text{ m} \times 30 \text{ m} =$ _____

13. $4 \text{ cm} \times$ _____ $= 56 \text{ cm}^2$

14. $20 \text{ cm} \times 20 \text{ cm} =$ _____

15. _____ $\times 70 \text{ m} = 140 \text{ m}^2$

Name _____ Date _____ Period _____

Using Metric Units to Find Volume

Directions Use the formula to find the volume of each figure.
Write your answer on the line. Include the unit in your answer.

volume = length × width × height

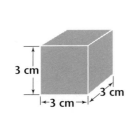

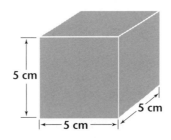

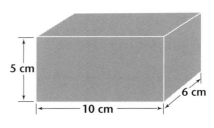

1. _____

2. _____

3. _____

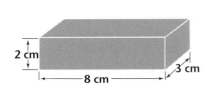

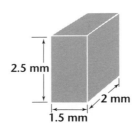

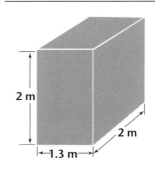

4. _____

5. _____

6. _____

Directions Write the volume of each box on the line. Be sure to include the unit in your answer.

7. 10 m × 10 m × 10 m =

_____

8. 1.5 cm × 1.5 cm × 1.5 cm =

_____

9. 4 mm × 4 mm × 4 mm =

_____

10. 240 m × 2 m × 150 m =

_____

11. 20 mm × 5 mm × 10 mm =

_____

12. 40 cm × 15 cm × 10 cm =

_____

13. 1.1 cm × 2 cm × 50 cm =

_____

14. 2 m × 3 m × 2 m =

_____

15. 225 cm × 150 cm × 50 cm =

_____

The Metric System: Terms Review

Directions Match each term in Column A with its meaning in Column B.
Write the correct letter on the line.

Column A	Column B
_____ **1.** area	**A** anything that has mass and takes up space
_____ **2.** balance	**B** a glass or plastic cylinder used to measure liquid volume
_____ **3.** meniscus	**C** a known amount used for measuring
_____ **4.** matter	**D** the basic unit of length in the metric system
_____ **5.** weight	**E** the curved surface of a liquid
_____ **6.** cubic centimeter	**F** a metric unit that means centimeter × centimeter × centimeter
_____ **7.** meter	
_____ **8.** displacement of water method	**G** an instrument used to measure mass
	H method of measuring volume of irregularly shaped objects
_____ **9.** exponent	**I** ordinary
_____ **10.** graduated cylinder	**J** the amount of space an object takes up
_____ **11.** volume	**K** a number that tells how many times another number is a factor
_____ **12.** metric system	
_____ **13.** customary	**L** the amount of material an object has
_____ **14.** unit	**M** system of measurement used by scientists
_____ **15.** mass	**N** the measure of how hard gravity pulls on an object
	O the amount of space the surface of an object takes up

Directions Write the abbreviation of the word in bold on the line.

_____ **16.** The are 1,000 **milliliters** in a liter.

_____ **17.** 1,000 meters is equal to a **kilometer**.

_____ **18.** A **milligram** is $\frac{1}{1,000}$ of a gram.

_____ **19.** A **meter** is equal to about 39 inches.

_____ **20.** A **centigram** is $\frac{1}{100}$ of a gram.

_____ **21.** One **kilogram** is about 2.2 pounds

_____ **22.** A **millimeter** is $\frac{1}{1,000}$ of a meter.

_____ **23.** The basic unit of mass in the metric system is the **gram**.

_____ **24.** A **liter** is slightly more than a quart.

_____ **25.** A **centimeter** is $\frac{1}{100}$ of a meter.

Properties of Objects

Directions Look at the objects below. On the lines, write properties that describe each object. Estimate each object's size, mass, and volume. Use the chart to help you choose units of measure.

	Volume of a Liquid	Volume of a Solid	Mass
Measured in	mL (milliliters) L (liters)	cm^3 (cubic centimeters) m^3 (cubic meters)	g (grams) kg (kilograms)
Examples	individual carton of milk is 237 mL water bottle is 500 mL	textbook is 1,500 cm^3	textbook is 1 kg

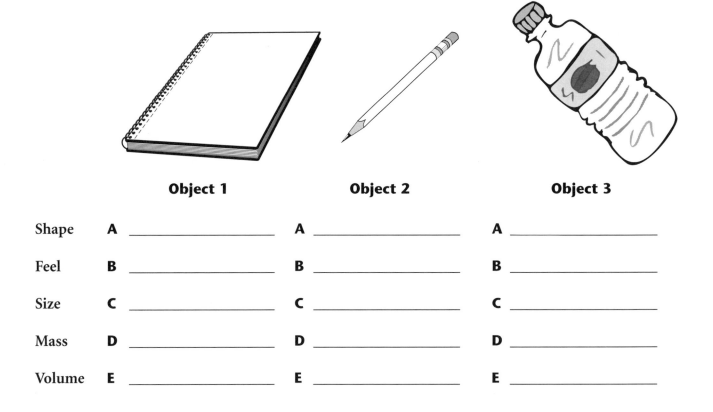

Object 1   **Object 2**   **Object 3**

Shape	**A** _____	**A** _____	**A** _____
Feel	**B** _____	**B** _____	**B** _____
Size	**C** _____	**C** _____	**C** _____
Mass	**D** _____	**D** _____	**D** _____
Volume	**E** _____	**E** _____	**E** _____

Identifying Solids, Liquids, and Gases

Directions Each figure below represents a different state of matter.
Use the figures to complete the following statements.

1. What are the smallest particles of a substance that have the same properties
as the substance?

They are _____.

2. Liquids are best represented by Figure _____.

3. Gases are best represented by Figure _____.

4. Figure _____ shows the state of matter with the greatest density.

5. One state of matter that is not represented by the figures is _____.

Figure A

Figure B

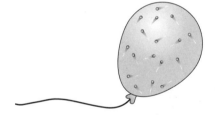

Figure C

Directions Match each item with the figure that best represents it.
Write the letter of the figure on the line.

6. ice cube _____

7. skateboard _____

8. feather _____

9. helium in
a balloon _____

10. raindrop _____

11. old ring _____

12. orange juice _____

13. bar of soap _____

14. air _____

15. water vapor from
a cooking pot _____

What Are Atoms Like?

Directions Label the model with letters *e*, *n*, and *p* to show its parts. The letter *e* stands for electron, *n* for neutron, and *p* for proton. Then complete each sentence about the model by writing an answer on the line.

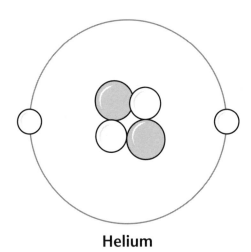

Helium

1. The model shows (a, an) _____ of helium.

2. The nucleus consists of _____

and _____.

3. The particles labeled *p* are _____.

4. The particles labeled *e* are _____.

5. The particles labeled *n* are _____.

Directions Complete the chart.

Element	Number of Protons	Number of Electrons
6. lithium	3	
7. boron		5
8. carbon		6
9. oxygen	8	
10. neon	10	

What Are Elements?

Directions Read the clues to complete the crossword puzzle. Each word is related to elements.

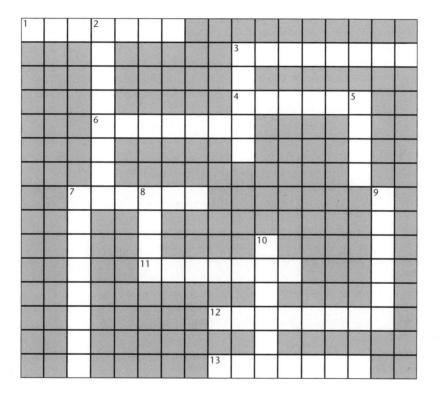

Across

1. matter that has only one kind of atom

3. an element used to make soft-drink cans

4. A water molecule contains one of these atoms.

6. an element that keeps bones healthy

7. an element used in some balloons

11. There are 92 of these elements.

12. an element used in fertilizers

13. an element used in thermometers

Down

2. A water _____ is made of three parts.

3. All of these are alike in the same element.

5. an element used in signs

7. There are two of these atoms in a water molecule.

8. one of the elements in steel

9. A pencil point has billions of these atoms.

10. takes up space and has mass

Words from Chemical Symbols

Directions Read the clue in Column A. You can find the answer from the elements in Column B. In Column C, write the symbols for the elements in Column B. The word you form should be the correct answer for the clue. The first one is done for you.

A	B	C
1. A farm animal	cobalt-tungsten	CoW
2. A musical group	barium-neodymium	
3. The opposite of *lose*	tungsten-iodine-nitrogen	
4. A building material	bromine-iodine-carbon-potassium	
5. Found on a door	potassium-nitrogen-oxygen-boron	
6. Used to write on a blackboard	carbon-hydrogen-aluminum-potassium	
7. A dog's sound	boron-argon-potassium	
8. It's 150 million km away	sulfur-uranium-nitrogen	
9. A source of energy	cobalt-aluminum	
10. A funny person	chlorine-oxygen-tungsten-nitrogen	
11. Used in hockey	plutonium-carbon-potassium	
12. Something to run in	radium-cerium	
13. A form of money	cobalt-iodine-nitrogen	
14. Show of affection	potassium-iodine-sulfur-sulfur	
15. Another word for *ill*	silicon-carbon-potassium	
16. An infant	barium-boron-yttrium	
17. A narrow street	lanthanum-neon	
18. To make better	helium-aluminum	
19. King of the beasts	lithium-oxygen-nitrogen	
20. A form of precipitation	radium-iodine-nitrogen	

Using the Periodic Table

Directions Write the atomic number for the element in each square. Then add the five atomic numbers in each row and in each column. Write the sums. If your atomic numbers are correct, the sums will all be the same.

Fe	As	Ne	Cl	Cr	Sums
___	___	___	___	___	___
Ge	Si	S	V	Mn	
___	___	___	___	___	___
Al	P	Ti	Cu	Ga	
___	___	___	___	___	___
K	Sc	Ni	Zn	Mg	
___	___	___	___	___	___
Ca	Co	Se	Na	Ar	
___	___	___	___	___	___

Sums

_____   _____   _____   _____   _____

The Structure of Matter: Terms Review

Directions Match each term in Column A with its meaning in Column B.
Write the letter on the line.

Column A	Column B
_____ **1.** tritium	**A** a particle found in the nucleus of an atom
_____ **2.** electron	**B** a particle with a negative charge
_____ **3.** atomic mass	**C** the form that matter has
_____ **4.** deuterium	**D** hydrogen isotope with one proton and one neutron
_____ **5.** neutron	**E** the average mass of all an element's isotopes
_____ **6.** state of matter	**F** hydrogen isotope with one proton and two neutrons
_____ **7.** isotope	**G** one of a group of atoms with the same number of electrons and protons
_____ **8.** symbol	**H** the central part of an atom
_____ **9.** nucleus	**I** an abbreviation for an element's name

Directions Unscramble the letters in parentheses to make a word that complete
each sentence. Write the word on the line.

10. A _____ is a substance made of two or more element combined chemically.
(modoncup)

11. A _____ is a particle with a positive charge in the nucleus of an atom. (troomp)

12. _____ is a characteristic that identifies an object. (tropepry)

13. _____ is the measure of how tightly packed matter in a given volume is.
(sendyti)

Directions Write an answer to each question.

14. How do the mass number and the atomic number of an element differ.

_____

15. How are natural elements different from other elements?

_____

_____

Physical and Chemical Changes

Directions Read each change listed in items 1 through 15. Write each change in the table. If it is a physical change, write the change in the left column. If it is a chemical change, write the change in the right column.

Physical Change	Chemical Change

1. scrambling eggs in a bowl
2. a silver spoon tarnishing
3. a puddle drying up
4. chopping onions
5. a copper roof turning green
6. water drops forming on the outside of a glass
7. bread baking

8. paper burning
9. picking tomatoes from a plant
10. mixing baking soda and vinegar
11. snow falling
12. painting a room
13. car-exhaust fumes mixing with water
14. adding a drink powder to water
15. bike spokes rusting

Directions How are physical changes and chemical changes different? Write your answer below.

_____

_____

_____

Energy Levels

Directions Write your answers on the lines.

1. How many electrons does the K level of an atom hold?   _____

2. How many electrons does the L level of an atom hold?   _____

3. How many electrons does the M level of an atom hold?   _____

4. How many electrons does the N level of an atom hold?   _____

5. What is the total number of electrons the four levels will hold?   _____

6. A hydrogen atom has 1 electron. In which level is it?   _____

7. A magnesium atom has 12 electrons. To what level are its electrons found?   _____

8. A zinc atom has 30 electrons. To what level are its electrons found?   _____

9. A nitrogen atom has 7 electrons. To what level are its electrons found?   _____

10. A sulfur atom has 16 electrons. To what level are its electrons found?   _____

11. A lithium atom has 3 electrons. To what level are its electrons found?   _____

12. An iron atom has 26 electrons. To what level are its electrons found?   _____

13. A mercury atom has 80 electrons. To what level are its electrons found?   _____

14. A zirconium atom has 40 electrons. To what level are its electrons found?   _____

15. A californium atom has 98 electrons. To what level are its electrons found?   _____

Directions Draw a magnesium atom. Show its energy levels and electrons.

Working with Chemical Formulas

Directions Write the chemical formula for each compound described. You can use the periodic table on pages 58–59 to find the chemical symbols.

1. silver chloride = one atom of silver + one atom of chlorine

_____

2. hydrochloric acid = one atom of hydrogen + one atom of chlorine

_____

3. hydrogen peroxide = two atoms of hydrogen + two atoms of oxygen

_____

4. magnesium carbonate = one atom of magnesium + one atom of carbon + three atoms of oxygen

_____

5. glucose = six atoms of carbon + twelve atoms of hydrogen + six atoms of oxygen

_____

6. lead nitrate = one atom of lead + two nitrate radicals

_____

Directions Complete the table. Write the names of the elements in each compound. Then write the number of atoms of each element.

Compound	Elements	Atoms
7. potassium chloride, KCl		
8. sucrose, $C_{12}H_{22}O_{11}$		
9. ammonium bromide, NH_4Br		
10. ammonium carbonate, $(NH_4)_2CO_3$		

Reactions and Solutions

Directions Write the best word for each description on the line.

1. person who tried to change various substances into gold _____

2. chemical change _____

3. part of a solution in which a substance dissolves _____

4. to break apart _____

5. a mixture in which one substance is dissolved in another _____

6. what you must apply to cause some chemical reactions _____

7. combination of substances in which no reaction occurs _____

8. what elements do in a reaction _____

9. the substance that is dissolved in a solution _____

10. what sugar breaks into when it is dissolved in water _____

Directions Write the answer to each question.

11. What is the difference between a mixture and a solution?

_____

_____

12. What is the difference between a solute and a solvent?

_____

_____

13. What is the difference between a mixture and a chemical reaction?

_____

_____

14. Name an example of a gas dissolved in a liquid.

_____

15. Name an example of a solution with a liquid solute and a solid solvent.

_____

Chemical Reactions: Terms Review

Directions Match each term in Column A with its meaning in Column B.
Write the letter on the line.

Column A	**Column B**
_____ **1.** dissolve	**A** a chemical change in which elements are combined or rearranged
_____ **2.** physical change	**B** to make the number of atoms the same on both sides of a chemical equation
_____ **3.** reactant	**C** a statement that uses symbols and formulas to describe a chemical reaction
_____ **4.** coefficient	**D** a substance that dissolves in solution
_____ **5.** chemical reaction	**E** a substance that changes in a chemical reaction
_____ **6.** chemical equation	**F** a number placed before a chemical formula to show the number of molecules
_____ **7.** solute	**G** a change in which appearance changes but chemical properties do not
_____ **8.** balance	**H** to break apart

Directions Unscramble the word or words in parentheses to complete each
sentence below.

9. A _____ level is one of the spaces in which electrons move around the nucleus
of an atom. (nyrege)

10. A _____ is the substance in which a solute dissolves. (novlest)

11. A _____ is one kind of mixture. (oilsnout)

12. The law of _____ of matter states that matter cannot be created or destroyed.
(introvosance)

13. A _____ is a substance that is formed during a reaction and shown on the right
side of a chemical equation. (cuptrod)

14. A _____ is a group of two or more atoms that acts like one atom. (slaidcar)

15. The 2 in H_2O is an example of a _____. (tripsbusc)

Energy

Directions Complete the web by naming the six forms of energy.

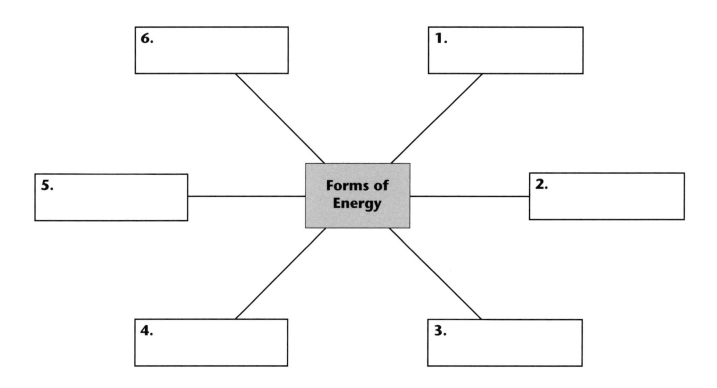

Directions Circle the term in parentheses that best completes the sentence.

7. Energy of motion is called (kinetic, potential).

8. A falling book has decreasing (potential, kinetic) energy.

9. When fuel is burned (radiant energy, chemical energy) converts to heat energy.

10. Steam is a form of (mechanical energy, heat energy).

Calculating Speed

EXAMPLE   To calculate average speed, divide the distance traveled by the elapsed time.

$$\text{average speed} = \frac{\text{distance}}{\text{time}}$$

distance	= 550 miles
elapsed time	= 10 hours
average speed	= 55 mi/hr

Directions   Calculate the average speed. Write the answer on the line.

1. distance = 120 millimeters \
    time = 60 seconds   _____

2. distance = 400 meters \
    time = 80 seconds   _____

3. distance = 700 centimeters \
    time = 35 seconds   _____

4. distance = 1,000 meters \
    time = 100 seconds   _____

5. distance = 175 miles \
    time = 5 hours   _____

6. distance = 12.5 millimeters \
    time = 0.5 seconds   _____

7. distance = 0.045 meters \
    time = 0.5 seconds   _____

8. distance = 0.015 millimeters \
    time = 0.10 seconds   _____

9. distance = 966 yards \
    time = 42 seconds   _____

10. distance = 396 kilometers \
    time = 6 hours   _____

Directions Read each word problem. Write the answer on the line.

11. If a runner goes 200 meters in 50 seconds, what is her average speed?   _____

12. If a train goes 846 miles in 9 hours, what is its average speed?   _____

13. A marathon runner can go 6 miles per hour. How long will it take him to run 26 miles?   _____

14. An airplane traveled for 5 hours at an average speed of 450 miles per hour. How far did it go?   _____

15. A car can average 52 miles per hour. How long will it take to go 416 miles?   _____

The Laws of Motion

Directions Read the clues. Then complete the puzzle.

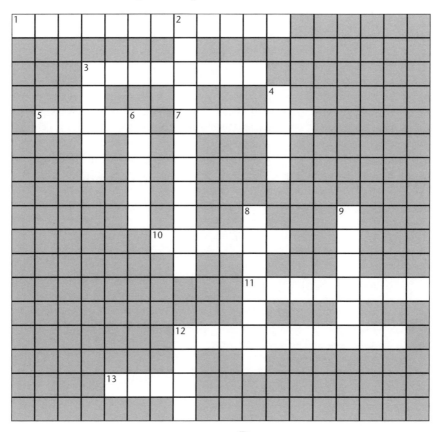

Across

1. force = mass × _____

3. a force that opposes motion

5. The _____ law of motion states that if no force acts on an object at rest, it will remain at rest.

7. This is a change in position.

10. The _____ law of motion describes the amount of force needed to change the motion of an object.

11. For every action, there is an equal and opposite _____.

12. One form of friction is air _____.

13. The amount of force needed to accelerate an object depends on the object's _____.

Down

2. Designers work to reduce air resistance on these.

3. a push or a pull

4. Friction is created when things slide or _____ over each other.

6. The _____ law of motion tells what happens when one object exerts a force on a second object.

8. the tendency of an object to resist changes in its motion

9. the scientist who proposed three laws to explain motion

12. If no force acts on a nonmoving object, it remains at _____.

Energy and Motion: Terms Review

Directions Match each term in Column A with its meaning in Column B.
Write the letter on the line.

Column A

_____ **1.** energy

_____ **2.** acceleration

_____ **3.** law of conservation of energy

_____ **4.** gravity

_____ **5.** kinetic energy

_____ **6.** force

_____ **7.** generator

_____ **8.** elapsed time

_____ **9.** motion

Column B

A the ability to do work

B a change in position

C device that converts mechanical energy to electrical energy

D the time that passes between one event and another

E a rate of change in velocity

F rule that states energy cannot be created or destroyed

G the force of attraction between any two objects that have mass

H energy of motion

I a push or a pull

Directions Unscramble the word or words in parentheses to complete each sentence.

10. The _____ of a moving object tells the direction of motion as well as the speed. (yetlovic)

11. _____ is stored energy. (lipottean ryegen)

12. The length of the path between two points is _____. (candetis)

13. The law of _____ states that gravity depends on mass and distance. (savenuril tatairoving)

Directions Tell how each pair is alike and different.

14. speed and velocity_____

_____

15. inertia and friction _____

_____

What Is Work?

Directions On the line, write the word or words that best complete the sentence.

1. When work is done, an object changes its _____.

2. Work is done when a force moves an object in the _____ of the force that is applied.

3. To measure work, you must _____ the force by the distance through which it acts.

4. Work is measured in newton-meters, or _____.

5. The formula for measuring work is _____.

Directions Use the formula *work = force × distance* to find each answer. Give the answer in joules.

6. Julie rolled a 2-kg ball down a ramp 10 meters long. (Remember, 1 kg = 9.8 newtons.) How much work was done? _____

7. Kevin lifted a 10-newton box a distance of 1.5 meters. How much work did he do? _____

8. A high jumper weighing 700 newtons jumps over a bar 2.0 meters high. What work does the high jumper do? _____

9. A mountain climber who weighs 900 newtons scales a 100-meter cliff. How much work does the climber do? _____

10. A parent uses a force of 300 newtons to pull a toddler in a wagon for 400 meters. How much work did the parent do? _____

11. Pushing a lawn mower requires a force of 200 newtons. If 4,000 joules of work is performed, how far has the mower moved? _____

12. A force of 550 newtons was used to move a stone 23 meters. How much work was done? _____

13. A box was pushed 42 meters, and 13,734 joules of work was done. How much force was used? _____

14. A pitcher threw a ball of 2 newtons and did 330 joules of work. How far did she throw the ball? _____

15. A landscape worker attempted to move a 300 kg boulder for 30 minutes but was unable to budge it. How much work did the worker do? _____

Using Levers

Directions Choose the word or words from the Word Bank that best complete each sentence.

Word Bank
effort force
fulcrum
lever
simple machine

1. A _____ is a tool that makes it easier to do work.

2. A _____ is a bar that moves about a fixed point.

3. The fixed point of a lever is its _____.

4. The force applied to a machine by a user is called the

_____.

Directions Use words from the box below to identify the type of lever and label its parts.

first-class lever	second-class lever	third-class lever
fulcrum	effort force (F_e)	resistance force (F_r)

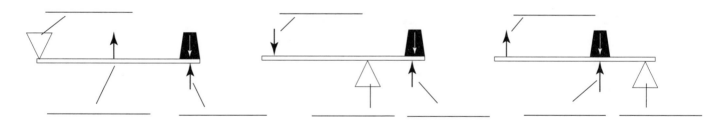

5. _____   **6.** _____   **7.** _____

Directions Calculate mechanical advantage.

8. Effort force = 5 newtons   Resistance force = 15 newtons: _____

9. Effort force = 10 newtons   Resistance force = 10 newtons: _____

10. Effort force = 6 newtons   Resistance force = 12 newtons: _____

Work and Machines: Terms Review

Directions Match each term in Column A with its meaning in Column B.
Write the letter on the line.

Column A

_____ **1.** neutron

_____ **2.** joule

_____ **3.** wheel and axle

_____ **4.** first-class lever

_____ **5.** screw

_____ **6.** energy

_____ **7.** broom

_____ **8.** simple machine

_____ **9.** fulcrum

_____ **10.** effort force

_____ **11.** pulley

_____ **12.** wheelbarrow

_____ **13.** work

Column B

A wheel with a rope, chain, or belt around it

B the fixed point around which a lever moves

C an example of a second-class lever

D the metric measure of force

E tool with few parts that makes work easier

F the metric unit of work

G the ability to do work

H an example of a third-class lever

I force × distance

J a lever with the fulcrum between the effort and resistance

K machine made of a wheel attached to a shaft

L the force a user applies to a machine

M a form of an inclined plane

Directions Unscramble the word or words in parentheses to complete
each sentence.

14. A simpler name for a neutron-meter is _____. (eloju)

15. A bar that rotates on a fulcrum is called a _____. (vreel)

16. The force applied to a machine by the object to be moved is called
the _____ force. (tressacine)

17. A _____ is an inclined plane that moves when it is used. (gweed)

18. Work is equal to _____ times force. (ticsnead)

19. The number of times a machine multiples your effort force is called
its _____ (acmehnlaic vnageadta)

20. A simple machine made of a ramp is an _____. (diinnelc leapn)

What Is Heat?

Directions Use the clues to complete the crossword puzzle. You may use your book for help.

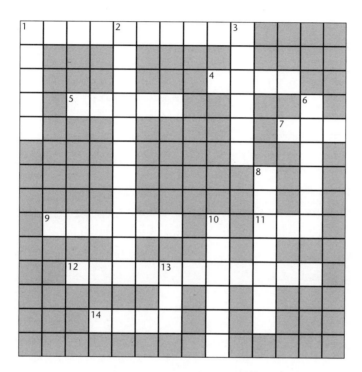

Across

1. a place from which heat energy comes (2 words)

4. a form of energy resulting from the motion of particles in matter

5. _____ shine because their atoms release nuclear energy.

7. _____ gases make a car's engine work.

9. the nuclear reaction that occurs when atoms are joined together

11. the earth's most important heat source

12. the heat source for a toaster

14. the size of the particles whose movement creates heat

Down

1. Rubbing your _____ together produces heat.

2. a machine that uses heated water to operate (2 words)

3. Heat is a form of _____.

6. Heat results from the _____ of atoms and molecules.

8. the reaction that occurs when an atom splits

10. the part of a steam engine that changes water to steam

13. The first steam engine was used as a _____.

How Heat Affects Matter

Directions Choose the word from the Word Bank that best completes each sentence. You will use one word twice.

Word Bank			
evaporates	condensation	expands	contracts

1. Matter generally _____ when you heat it.

2. Water _____ when you boil it.

3. That frost on your window is an example of _____.

4. Water _____ when it becomes ice.

5. When particles in matter move more slowly, the matter usually _____.

Directions Each sentence tells about a process that is occurring. Write the letter of the process that is occurring on the line.

A liquid to solid   **B** liquid to gas   **C** solid to liquid   **D** gas to liquid

_____ **6.** A can of a soft drink in the freezer bursts.

_____ **7.** The bathroom walls are covered with water after your shower.

_____ **8.** The water in the teakettle is bubbling.

_____ **9.** The rain puddle is getting smaller.

_____ **10.** The ice cream is running down the cone.

Directions Complete the following sentences.

11. Cold air cannot hold as much _____ as warm air.

12. Molecules in a _____ move more freely than in a liquid.

13. Bubbles in boiling water are made up of water _____.

14. In the _____ months, a metal bridge is likely to expand.

15. One familiar material that does not contract when it gets colder is _____.

Temperature

Directions Write the correct word for each definition on the line. To check your answers, find each vocabulary word in the puzzle below.

1. a type of energy caused by the motion of molecules _____

2. results from a change at the melting point _____

3. results from a change at the boiling point _____

4. a measure of the average motion of the molecules in a substance _____

5. a device that measures temperature _____

6. the temperature scale on which water boils at 212° _____

7. the temperature scale used for scientific work _____

8. the temperature at which a solid changes to a liquid (2 words) _____

9. what water does at 100°C _____

10. the unit for measuring temperature _____

11. what water does at 32°F _____

12. a substance commonly used in antifreeze _____

13. to change from °F to °C, or vice versa _____

14. what state a substance becomes at freezing point _____

15. a liquid metal sometimes used in thermometers _____

```
G  B  O  I  L  S  D  L  Q  V  N  P  S  O  E
Y  Z  Q  Q  W  E  R  J  K  K  C  C  L  R  V
H  T  H  K  O  I  B  I  S  E  T  U  U  M  C
N  I  E  E  I  S  L  F  L  A  I  T  R  E  O
B  E  A  I  A  R  N  S  P  A  A  T  R  L  N
I  H  C  G  K  T  I  S  H  R  A  N  H  T  V
Y  N  B  E  L  U  E  E  E  R  G  E  D  I  E
R  E  A  N  S  Z  Y  P  V  S  P  M  I  N  R
U  R  M  P  E  S  M  S  V  Y  C  F  I  G  T
C  H  J  E  G  E  D  O  A  X  U  R  O  P  N
R  A  R  L  T  A  B  L  A  L  C  O  H  O  L
E  F  C  E  G  J  D  I  U  Q  I  L  L  I  U
M  A  F  S  M  Q  C  D  O  X  W  B  A  N  C
T  T  H  E  R  M  O  M  E  T  E  R  T  T  L
A  E  H  W  U  V  F  N  I  L  F  B  V  R  N
```

Heat: Terms Review

Directions Match each term in Column A with its meaning in Column B.
Write the correct letter on the line.

Column A

_____ **1.** expand

_____ **2.** temperature

_____ **3.** degree

_____ **4.** Fahrenheit scale

_____ **5.** evaporate

_____ **6.** melting point

_____ **7.** nuclear fission

_____ **8.** freezing point

_____ **9.** Celsius scale

_____ **10.** nuclear fusion

_____ **11.** thermometer

_____ **12.** boiling point

_____ **13.** contract

_____ **14.** heat

Column B

A to change from a liquid to a gas

B a form of energy resulting from the motion of particles in matter

C temperature at which a solid changes into a liquid

D the reaction occurring when the nucleus of an atom splits

E a measure of how fast an object's particles are moving

F a device that measures temperature

G the temperature scale in which water freezes at 0°

H the temperature at which a substance changes to a gas

I a unit of measurement on a temperature scale

J the reaction occurring when atoms are joined together

K the temperature scale commonly used in the United States

L to become larger in size

M the temperature at which a liquid changes to a solid

N to become smaller in size

Directions Unscramble the word in parentheses to complete each sentence.

15. The flow of heat energy through matter by molecules bumping into

each other is _____. (noitcudonc)

16. Copper is an excellent _____ of heat energy. (rotnocduc)

17. Energy from the sun reaches us by _____. (idiotrana)

18. Warm liquids rise as a result of _____. (nevoncocit)

19. A _____ is space without matter. (camuvu)

20. A material that does not conduct heat well is called an _____. (sularotin)

What Is Sound?

Directions Choose the term from the box that completes each sentence.

1. For a sound to occur, matter must _____,
   or move back and forth.

2. Vibration of an object causes _____
   to compress and expand many times.

3. Air moves out in all directions from a vibrating object as a
   _____.

4. You may not see these waves, but you can hear the resulting
   _____.

5. Sounds grow fainter over distance because the sound waves become
   _____ the farther they travel from the
   vibrating object.

molecules
sound wave
sounds
vibrate
weaker

Directions Look at the figures below. Write a sentence or two that explains how the movement of the wire spring is like sound waves.

_____

_____

_____

Directions Write the answer to the question on the lines.

You toss a stone into water, and ripples spread out from where it hits.
How are these ripples like sound waves?

_____

_____

_____

What Is Light?

Directions Choose the word or words from the box that best complete each sentence.

wavelengths
empty space
light
photons
prism
visible spectrum

1. The sun is a major source of _____ on Earth.

2. Light is made up of atoms in energy bundles called

    _____.

3. Light waves travel fastest through _____.

4. A _____ can separate white light into colors of the

    _____.

5. The sun's energy arrives as light with a range of _____.

Directions Write the colors of the visible spectrum in the order they appear. Then complete the sentence.

6. _____   9. _____   11. _____

7. _____   10. _____   12. _____

8. _____

13. When white light passes through a prism, it _____

    _____

    _____.

Directions Circle the answer that best completes each sentence.

14. Light travels fastest through _____

    A solids   **B** liquids   **C** empty space   **D** gas

15. Light waves travel _____ sound waves

    A more slowly than   **C** at the same speed as

    B more quickly than   **D** next to

Sound and Light: Terms Review

Directions Match each term in Column A with its meaning in Column B.
Write the letter on the line.

Column A

_____ **1.** photon

_____ **2.** farsighted person

_____ **3.** image

_____ **4.** plane mirror

_____ **5.** prism

_____ **6.** nearsighted person

_____ **7.** refraction

_____ **8.** light

_____ **9.** reflection

_____ **10.** lens

Column B

A a glass with a triangular shape that can separate white light

B the bending of light as it passes through a material

C bouncing back of a light wave

D form of energy that can be seen

E uses glasses with concave lenses

F curved piece of clear material that refracts light waves

G a flat, smooth, clear reflecting surface

H a copy or likeness

I tiny bundles of energy that make up light

J uses glasses with convex lenses

Directions Unscramble the word or words in parentheses to complete each sentence.

11. The sun is the major source of _____ on the earth. (thilg)

12. A(n) _____ curves inward in the middle. (venocca rimror)

13. White light can be split into the _____. (blisive crumptes)

14. In order for sound to occur, matter must _____. (tearbiv)

15. Sound waves become _____ as they move away from the vibrating object. (rewake)

16. A _____ produces sound waves when it is struck. (nutign krof)

17. A _____ helps correct nearsightedness. (navecoc snel)

18. A _____ curves outward at the middle. (coxven roirmr)

19. A _____ is produced by vibrations. (dunso evwa)

20. A _____ refracts light waves inward. (xevocn nels)

How Electricity Flows

Directions Write the correct word or words for each definition on the line.
Then circle the word in the puzzle below.

1. a discharge of static electricity from a cloud   _____

2. a complete, unbroken path for electric current   _____

3. an incomplete path for electric current   _____

4. flow of electrons   _____

5. Electricity is a form of _____.   _____

6. kind of diagram that uses symbols to show parts of a circuit   _____

7. unit that tells how much electric current flows through a wire   _____

8. We measure electric _____ in amperes.   _____

9. where an electric circuit begins   _____

10. kind of electricity caused by a buildup of charge   _____

```
P  B  C  C  S  D  V  I  V  U  K  R  O  U  B  E  E
T  H  P  D  A  E  S  F  D  S  T  A  T  I  C  L  L
N  A  Z  E  N  E  R  G  Y  J  I  A  U  O  Y  E  P
E  R  U  M  I  C  E  A  G  S  L  M  Z  A  Z  C  S
R  A  T  I  E  U  C  N  X  R  V  P  T  O  H  T  C
R  L  A  K  S  Q  I  P  L  F  M  E  I  T  K  R  H
U  L  Y  M  C  N  O  E  X  U  T  R  R  M  A  I  E
C  E  W  W  T  M  P  R  Y  T  N  E  V  F  H  C  M
E  L  E  H  R  P  T  E  O  I  S  K  U  S  P  I  A
P  C  G  V  E  O  P  E  N  C  I  R  C  U  I  T  T
C  I  N  R  U  R  D  N  J  G  H  E  P  N  O  Y  I
L  R  O  O  I  E  Q  T  O  O  C  B  R  N  T  F  C
J  C  L  O  S  E  D  C  I  R  C  U  I  T  H  S  O
A  F  C  P  D  X  I  O  N  S  P  N  T  S  G  P  T
R  Q  L  T  E  C  R  U  O  S  R  E  W  O  P  Y  N
C  N  T  O  R  L  D  H  W  Y  T  R  I  F  D  P  X
```

Series Circuits

Directions Label the parts of the series circuit. Identify the *power source*, *wire*, *switch*, and *bulb* in the diagram of the series circuit. Draw arrows to show the direction of the electron flow.

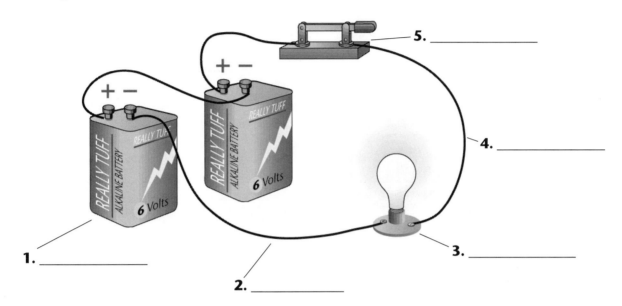

5. _____

4. _____

3. _____

1. _____

2. _____

Directions Choose an item from the box to complete each sentence.

| add | disadvantage | fires | not work | series |
| circuit breaker | 15 | fuse | one | voltage |

6. In a series circuit, electrons flow through _____ path.

7. One _____ of a series circuit is that all lights go out if one goes out.

8. If another electrical device were added to the circuit shown above, the _____ would be lower in each device.

9. To find the voltage of a series circuit, _____ the voltages of the cells.

10. If a series circuit had 3 batteries and each had 5 volts, the circuit would have a total of _____ volts.

11. The batteries of a flashlight often have a _____ circuit.

12. If one battery in a flashlight does not work, the flashlight will _____.

13. Fuses and circuit breakers prevent _____.

14. A _____ works by melting and breaking a circuit with hot wires.

15. A _____ switches off a circuit if it gets too hot.

Parallel Circuits

Directions The chart shows how a parallel circuit compares to a series circuit.
Read the information, then complete the chart.

	Series Circuit	**Parallel Circuit**
1. Number of paths it has	one	
2. Advantages	Batteries in a series deliver more energy in the same amount of time.	
3. Disadvantages	If one light goes out, they all go out.	
4. What happens when electrical devices are added to the circuit?	Voltage is lowered in each device.	
5. What is the total voltage of batteries in the circuit?	total voltages of all the cells	

Directions Tell how many paths are in this parallel circuit.

6. _____

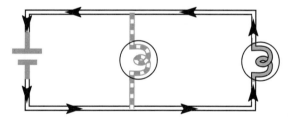

Directions Look at the 2 diagrams. Label one diagram *series circuit* and the other one *parallel circuit*.
Then write the total voltage of each circuit.

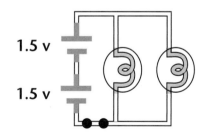

1.5 v

1.5 v

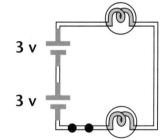

3 v

3 v

7. _____

9. Total voltage: _____

8. _____

10. Total voltage: _____

What Are Magnets?

Directions Read the clues. Then complete the puzzle.

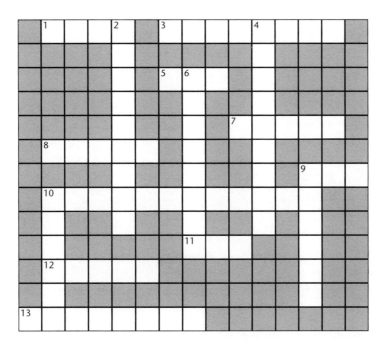

Across

1. Opposite poles of a magnet _____ together.

3. This magnet is shaped like something you can eat!

5. This animal sometimes swallows a magnet for its health.

7. Poles of the same type _____ each other.

8. the magnetic pole represented by the letter S

9. a machine that uses magnetism to view the human body

10. the end of a magnet (2 words)

11. A magnetic pole is located on each _____ of a bar magnet.

12. the magnetic pole represented by the letter N

13. The south pole of one magnet _____ the north pole of another.

Down

2. also known as *magnetite*

4. a magnet shaped like the letter U

6. _____ poles attract each other.

9. Magnets attract certain kinds of _____, such as iron.

10. it comes in several common shapes

Identifying a Magnetic Field

Directions Look at the two pairs of bar magnets. The broken lines represent their lines of force. Beside the numbers 1 through 8, write the letters *N* or *S*, for north pole or south pole. (Hint: There is more than one possible solution.)

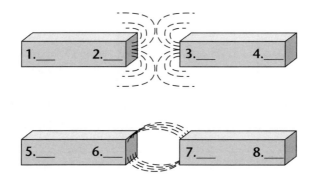

1.___ 2.___   3.___ 4.___

5.___ 6.___   7.___ 8.___

Directions Use words from the word box to complete the paragraph.

Earth	field	lights	pole	sun

9. _____ is like a giant magnet. It has a north and a south

magnetic **10.** _____. Like a magnet, the earth's magnetic

11. _____ is strongest at the poles. Electrically charged

particles from the **12.** _____ get trapped at the earth's poles.

They collide with molecules to create the spectacular northern **13.** _____.

Directions Write your answers to the questions on the lines.

14. Explain how you could use iron filings and a piece of paper to help reveal the effect of a magnetic field.

_____

_____

15. Why does the north pole of a compass point towards the earth's north magnetic pole?

_____

_____

Electricity and Magnetism: Terms Review

Directions Match each term in Column A with its meaning in Column B. Write
the letter on the line.

Column A

_____ 1. open circuit

_____ 2. electromagnet

_____ 3. magnet

_____ 4. series circuit

_____ 5. closed circuit

_____ 6. motor

_____ 7. parallel circuit

_____ 8. circuit

_____ 9. magnetic field

_____ 10. repel

_____ 11. schematic diagram

_____ 12. electricity

_____ 13. attract

_____ 14. magnetic pole

_____ 15. electric current

_____ 16. static electricity

Column B

A a type of circuit having more than one path for current

B an object that attracts certain kinds of metal

C a device that converts electrical energy to mechanical energy

D an unbroken path for electric current

E push apart

F a type of circuit having only one path for current

G temporary magnet uses a current to magnetize

H area in which magnetic forces can act

I an incomplete path for electric current

J a path for electric current

K pull together

L buildup of electrical charge

M an illustration that uses symbols to show the parts of a circuit

N movement of electrons from one place to another

O flow of electrons

P the end of a magnet, where magnetic forces are greatest

Directions Unscramble the word or words in parentheses to complete
each sentence.

17. An _____ is the unit used to describe the amount of current flowing
through a wire. (parmere)

18. _____ is the relationship between magnetism and electricity.
(gametimeclonster)

19. The _____ on an open circuit is open. (twchsi)

20. _____ can travel on more than one path in a parallel circuit. (stonecrel)

Unit 2

The Earth's Features

Directions 1–11. Look at the map of the earth. Label each of the seven continents on the map. Then label each of the four oceans.

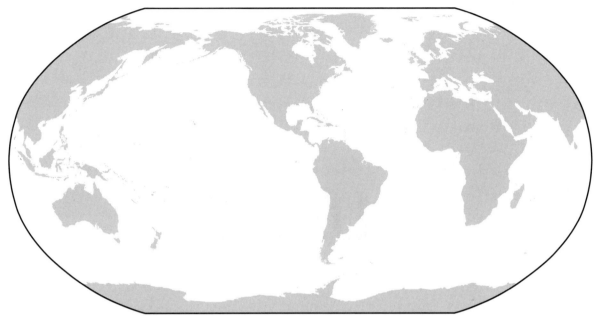

Directions Answer the questions.

12. Which continent is the smallest? _____

13. Which ocean is the largest? _____

14. In kilometers, how much larger is the distance around the earth from east to west than the distance from north to south? _____

15. What percent of the earth's land area does North America cover? _____

16. Which ocean is the deepest? _____

17. Why might the earth's oceans be described as one huge ocean?

_____

18. Which continents are not connected to other continents?

_____

19. Besides distance, why can't you see across an ocean to land on the other side?

_____

20. Use the circle to draw a circle graph that shows how much of the earth is water and how much is land.

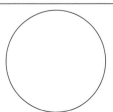

The Earth's Rotation and Time

Directions For each pair of cities below, use the time zone map to figure out the time in the second city. Write the time on the line. Be sure to include A.M. or P.M.

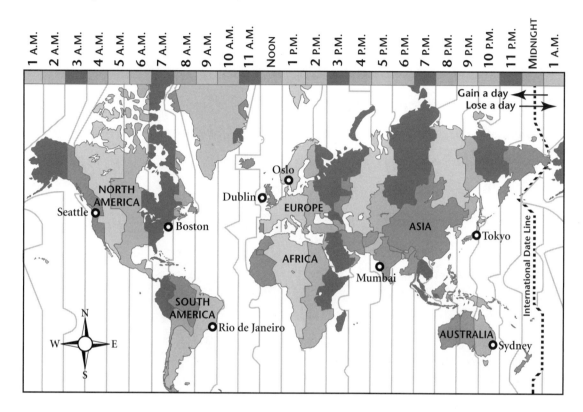

1. 4:00 P.M.   Boston, Massachusetts
_____   Sydney, Australia

2. 1:00 A.M.   Rio de Janeiro, Brazil
_____   Tokyo, Japan

3. 11:00 P.M.   Mumbai, India
_____   Dublin, Ireland

4. 8:00 A.M.   Oslo, Norway
_____   Seattle, Washington

5. 12:00 NOON   Seattle, Washington
_____   Rio de Janeiro, Brazil

6. 2:00 P.M.   Sydney, Australia
_____   Mumbai, India

7. 9:00 P.M.   Oslo, Norway
_____   Dublin, Ireland

8. 2:00 P.M.   Mumbai, India
_____   Rio de Janeiro, Brazil

Directions Answer the questions.

9. In hours, what is the time difference between Boston and Rio de Janeiro? _____

10. If you traveled from Oslo to Tokyo, would you move your watch forward or backward?

_____

The Earth's Movement in Space

Directions Write the term from the Word Bank that best completes each sentence.

1. One orbit around an object is one _____.

2. The earth revolves around the sun once a _____.

3. A sphere spins one time; this equals one _____.

4. The earth rotates on its axis once a _____.

5. Seasons occur because the earth revolves and is _____ on its axis.

6. The angle of tilt of the earth's _____ is exactly 23.5 degrees.

7. The part of the earth that is tilted toward the sun is having _____.

8. This happens because the sun's rays strike the earth more _____ then.

9. The part of the earth that is tilted away from the sun has _____.

10. There is less heat when the sun's rays strike the earth at an _____.

Word Bank
angle
axis
day
directly
revolution
rotation
summer
tilted
winter
year

Directions Use the diagram on page 226 of the textbook to complete the table below.
For angle of light, write *direct*, *in between*, or *indirect*.
Parts of the chart have been filled in.

Hemisphere	Date	Angle of Light	Season
Northern	December 21	**11.**	**12.**
Southern	December 21	**13.**	**14.**
Northern	March 21	**15.**	**16.**
Southern	March 21	in between	fall
Northern	June 21	direct	summer
Southern	June 21	indirect	winter
Northern	September 23	**17.**	**18.**
Southern	September 23	**19.**	**20.**

A Grid System on a Globe: Terms Review

Directions Read the clues to complete the puzzle.

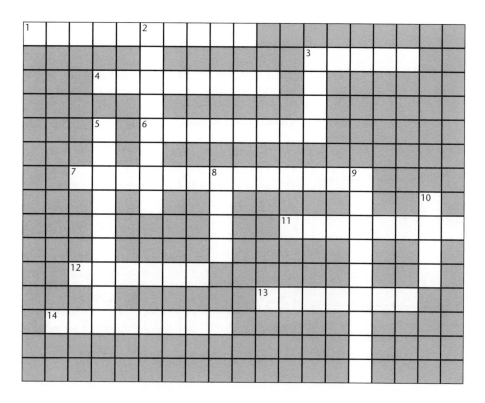

Across

1. half of the earth

3. _____ meridian: line of 0° longitude

4. line of longitude

6. angle that describes the distance north or south of the equator

7. _____ date line: marks the place on the earth where each new day begins

11. _____ time zone: an area that has the same clock time

12. unit for measuring angles in a circle or sphere

13. line of 0° latitude

14. spinning of the earth

Down

2. line of latitude

3. point that the earth's axis passes through

5. one of the seven major land areas of the earth

8. imaginary line through the earth

9. angle that describes the distance east or west of the prime meridian

10. set of horizontal and vertical lines on a map

Properties Used to Identify Minerals

Directions Look at the concept map of mineral properties. Match each empty box in the map with an answer from the Answer Bank. Write the letter of the correct answer in the box.

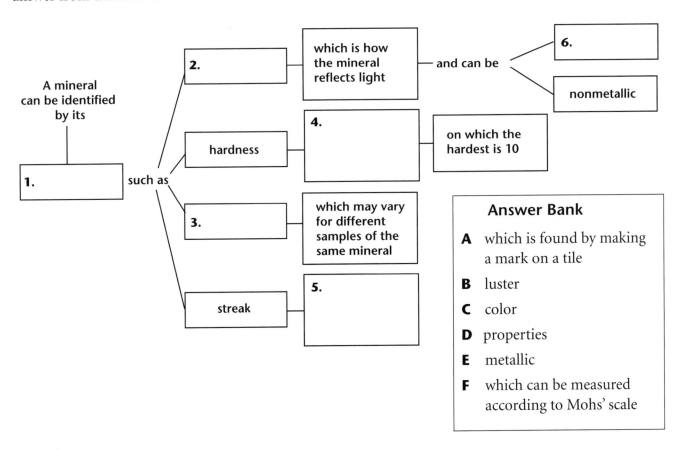

Answer Bank

A which is found by making a mark on a tile

B luster

C color

D properties

E metallic

F which can be measured according to Mohs' scale

Directions Unscramble the word in parentheses to complete each sentence. Write the answer on the line.

7. _____ and pyrite may look alike, but their streaks are different. (dolg)

8. No other mineral is capable of scratching a _____. (donmaid)

9. One of the very softest minerals is _____. (lact)

10. Mohs' scale measures _____. (sendrash)

11. The _____ of quartz is described as glassy. (elrust)

12. A hard mineral can scratch a _____ one. (fots)

13. Sulfur is easy to recognize because it is bright _____. (wolley)

14. When doing a streak test, use a _____ tile. (thwie)

15. You can quickly test for hardness by using a copper _____. (nynep)

The Rock Cycle: Terms Review

Directions: Match each term with its definition. Write the letter of the correct definition on the line.

_____ **1.** intrusive rock
_____ **2.** metamorphic rock
_____ **3.** rock
_____ **4.** hardness
_____ **5.** igneous rock
_____ **6.** carbon
_____ **7.** sedimentary rock
_____ **8.** mineral
_____ **9.** rock cycle
_____ **10.** extrusive rock
_____ **11.** sediment
_____ **12.** streak
_____ **13.** luster
_____ **14.** Mohs' scale
_____ **15.** magma

A natural changes that cause one form of rock to become another
B ability of mineral to resist being scratched
C element or compound found in the earth
D igneous rock that forms on the earth's surface
E solid particles that that forms layers at the bottom of an ocean or lake
F how a mineral reflects light
G rock formed by intense heat and pressure
H color of mark a mineral makes on a white tile
I rock formed as melted rock cools and hardens
J hot, liquid rock inside the earth
K graphite and diamonds are made up of this element
L natural, solid mixture of minerals
M rock formed by cementing layers of sediment
N igneous rock formed underground from cooled magma
O chart used to measure the hardness of minerals

Directions The Word Bank lists some forces that change rocks. Write the terms from the Word Bank on the correct lines in the diagram.

20. _____ Sediment **16.** _____
_____
Igneous rock
Sedimentary rock
19. _____
17. _____
_____
Magma
Metamorphic rock
18. _____

Word Bank
compacting and cementing
cooling and hardening
heat and pressure
melting
weathering and erosion

Weathering

Directions Look at the diagram of soil layers. Then name and describe each numbered layer in the table.

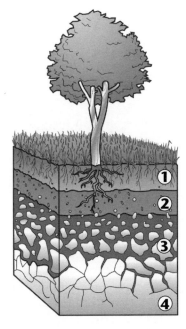

Layer Name	Description
1.	**5.**
2.	**6.**
3.	**7.**
4.	**8.**

Directions Match the term with its definition. Write the letter of the correct definition on the line.

_____ **9.** weathering

_____ **10.** mechanical weathering

_____ **11.** chemical weathering

_____ **12.** soil

A breaking down of rocks without changing their chemical makeup

B mixture of rock pieces and the remains of dead plants and animals

C breaking down of rocks on the earth's surface

D breaking down of rocks by changing their chemical makeup

Directions Write the answer to each item below.

13. Name three factors in the environment that cause weathering. _____

_____

14. Describe two examples of mechanical weathering. _____

_____

_____

15. Describe two examples of chemical weathering. _____

_____

Erosion by Water

Directions Read the clues to complete the puzzle.

Across

1. dropping of eroded sediment

4. area of land that is much like a delta

5. waves change this through erosion and deposition

7. curved finger of sand sticking out into the water

8. area where waves deposit sand, pebbles, or shells

11. an alluvial fan can form at the base of this landform

12. a major agent or erosion that has tributaries

Down

1. Fan-shaped area of land formed by deposition where a river empties into a lake or an ocean

2. place where a river flows into a larger body of water

3. an agent of erosion that pounds against shorelines

5. offshore underwater deposit of sand

6. the wearing away and moving of weathered rock and soil

7. tower of rock remaining after the top of an arch collapses

9. formed when waves erode through cliffs

10. eroded materials that drop out first as a river slows down

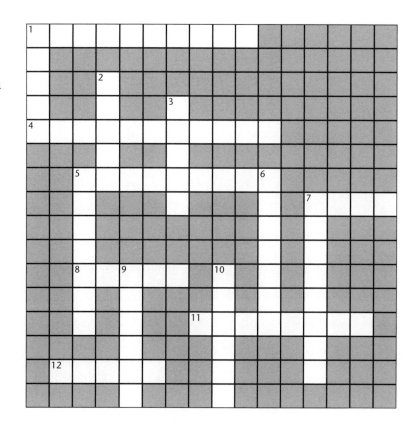

Glaciers

Directions Write the term from the word bank that best completes each sentence.

Word Bank					
basins	deposits	fjords	gravity	grooves	sandpaper
boulders	evidence	glacier	Great Lakes	moraines	snowfall

1. A _____ is a thick mass of ice that covers a large area.

2. The weight of snow and ice and the pull of _____ cause a glacier to move slowly downhill.

3. For a glacier to form, there must be a year-round low temperatures and heavy _____.

4. Huge _____ and soil freeze to the bottom and sides of a glacier.

5. Small rocks in glaciers act like _____, smoothing and shaping the land.

6. Large rocks in the bottom of a glacier can cut long _____ in the surface rock.

7. As ice in a glacier melts, the glacier _____ sediments.

8. Deposited sediments from glaciers form ridges called _____.

9. The moraines are the "footprints," or _____ that tells us that glaciers were here.

10. The _____ of Norway are U-shaped glacial valleys that are partly filled with ocean water.

11. Some glaciers carved wide, deep _____ that filled with water.

12. The _____ are examples of basins dammed by moraines and filled with water.

Directions Write the letter under the correct picture to tell how glaciers form some lakes.

A The ice block gets partly buried in sediment.
B An ice block breaks off a glacier.
C The ice block melts to form a lake.

13. _____

14. _____

15. _____

Erosion and Deposition: Terms Review

Directions Match each term with its definition. Write the letter of the correct definition on the line.

Column A	Column B
_____ **1.** alluvial fan	**A** breaking down of rocks on earth's surface
_____ **2.** chemical weathering	**B** fan-shaped land made from deposits where a mountain stream moves onto flat land
_____ **3.** delta	**C** ridge of sediment deposited by a glacier
_____ **4.** deposition	**D** breaking up of rocks caused by a change in their chemical makeup
_____ **5.** erosion	**E** wearing away and moving of weathered rock and soil
_____ **6.** glacier	**F** mixture of tiny pieces of weathered rock and remains of plants and animals
_____ **7.** mechanical weathering	**G** process in which minerals combine with oxygen to form new substances
_____ **8.** moraine	**H** layer of soil directly below the topsoil
_____ **9.** mouth	**I** layer of soil that is rich in oxygen and organic material
_____ **10.** oxidation	**J** fan-shaped land formed when sediment is deposited where a river empties into a lake or an ocean
_____ **11.** soil	**K** place where a river flows into a larger body of water
_____ **12.** subsoil	**L** breaking apart of rocks without changes in their mineral content
_____ **13.** topsoil	**M** dropping of eroded sediment
_____ **14.** weathering	**N** thick mass of ice that covers a large area

Directions Answer the question.

15. Tell how a sand dune and an alluvial fan are alike. Tell how they are different.

_____

_____

_____

Movement of the Earth's Crust

Directions Write each phrase from the Answer Bank under the part of the earth it describes.

Answer Bank

8 to 70 kilometers thick	innermost layer	iron and nickel
2,900 kilometers thick	outer layer	churning, hot rock
3,500 kilometers thick	middle layer	continents and ocean floor

Crust

1. _____

2. _____

3. _____

Mantle

4. _____

5. _____

6. _____

Core

7. _____

8. _____

9. _____

Directions Write the terms from the Word Bank that best complete the sentences.

10. Alfred Wegener believed all of the continents on the earth were joined

millions of years ago as one landmass called _____.

11. The surface of the earth's crust is made of large _____,

which _____, _____,
or slide past each other.

12. The earth's plates move because the magma beneath them has

_____ currents, or circular motion.

Word Bank

collide

convection

move apart

Pangaea

plates

Directions Explain each theory on the lines below.

13. continental drift _____

_____

_____

14. sea-floor spreading _____

_____

_____

15. plate tectonics _____

_____

_____

Volcanoes

Directions Write each answer from the Answer Bank in the correct part of the table.

Answer Bank		
both explosions and quiet flows	loose rock particles	small and steep
explosive blasts	low and broad	tall
lava layers and rocky layers	quiet flows	thin lava layers

Type of Volcano	Type of Eruption	Type of Material	Shape
cinder cone	**1.**	**2.**	**3.**
shield	**4.**	**5.**	**6.**
composite	**7.**	**8.**	**9.**

Directions Write the term from the Word Bank that best completes each sentence.

10. Volcanoes form because magma rises through openings called

_____.

11. Most volcanoes form where two _____ meet.

12. A small volcano built of loose rock particles is called a(n)

_____.

13. Shield volcanoes form from thin basalt lava, so their eruptions are not very

_____.

14. Composite volcanoes form from alternating explosive eruptions and

_____ eruptions of lava.

15. _____ volcanoes have a broad shape.

Word Bank
cinder cone
explosive
plates
quiet
shield
vents

Mountains

Directions Write each answer from the Answer Bank in the correct part of the table.

Answer Bank
• Cascade Range
• Continental plates collide, bending rock layers.
• The earth's crust breaks, and blocks of rock rise.
• fault
• folding
• Grand Tetons
• Himalayas
• One plate sinks beneath another or two plates separate.
• volcanic

Ways Mountains Form		
Type of Formation	**Force Causing Formation**	**Example**
1.	2.	3.
4.	5.	6.
7.	8.	9.

Directions **10–15.** Draw lines to connect each fault diagram with its name on the left and its description on the right.

strike-slip fault

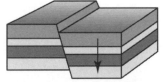

Overhanging block of rock is raised.

normal fault

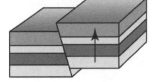

Blocks of rock slide past each other.

reverse fault

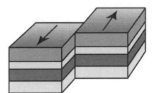

Overhanging block of rock slides down.

Earthquakes: Terms Review

Directions Draw lines to connect each earthquake wave with its description.

1. P-wave   fastest, causes rocks to vibrate back and forth

2. L-wave   slower, causes rocks to vibrate up and down

3. S-wave   slowest, causes the ground to twist and bend

Directions Match each term with its definition. Write the letter of the correct definition on the line.

____ 4. focus
____ 5. epicenter
____ 6. Pangaea
____ 7. seismograph
____ 8. volcano
____ 9. plate tectonics
____ 10. tsunami
____ 11. folding
____ 12. sea-floor spreading
____ 13. continental drift
____ 14. vent
____ 15. convection current
____ 16. earthquake
____ 17. Richter

A theory that the earth's landmasses move

B circular motion of a gas or liquid as it heats

C earthquake's origin inside the earth

D mountain formed when magma erupts

E shaking of the earth's crust

F theory that the earth's crust is made of moving sections

G large ocean wave caused by an earthquake

H point directly over the focus of an earthquake

I theory that new crust forms at mid-ocean ridges

J name of the scale that measures earthquake strength

K instrument that detects earthquake waves

L opening at the top of a volcano

M process in which rock layers bend under pressure

N single landmass that separated into continents

Directions Write the terms from the Word Bank in the correct boxes below.

Word Bank				
cinder cone	core	mantle	reverse	strike-slip
composite	crust	normal	shield	

18. Faults	19. Volcanoes	20. The Earth's Layers
• _____	• _____	• _____
• _____	• _____	• _____
• _____	• _____	• _____

The Rock Record

Directions Find the lettered phrase that best completes each sentence. Write the letter of the correct phrase on the line.

_____ **1.** To find out about the earth's past, scientists ___.

_____ **2.** Because of fossils, we know that ___.

_____ **3.** Organisms that are buried quickly after death ___.

_____ **4.** When animals become trapped in tree sap, their ___.

_____ **5.** Hard ___ do not decay easily and may become fossils.

_____ **6.** All of the time since the earth's formation is ___.

_____ **7.** Petrification occurs when minerals replace ___.

_____ **8.** A fossil is the remains of an organism ___.

_____ **9.** A mold is the ___ where an organism was buried.

_____ **10.** If minerals fill a mold, ___.

A certain organisms once existed

B space left in a rock

C study rock layers and fossils

D can become fossils

E a cast forms

F geologic time

G a buried organism

H preserved in the earth's crust

I teeth, bones, and shells

J actual bodies can be preserved

Directions Match each fossil description with one of the three terms below. Write *P*, *I*, or *T* on the line.

P petrification	**I** imprint (mold or cast)	**T** trapped and preserved

_____ **11.** A mosquito is caught in amber.

_____ **12.** A trilobite decays, leaving an imprint.

_____ **13.** A saber-toothed tiger falls in a tar pit.

_____ **14.** The wood in a tree branch is replaced by minerals.

_____ **15.** Minerals fill the mold of a seashell.

_____ **16.** A log turns into minerals.

_____ **17.** A leaf decays and leaves its shape in the sediment.

_____ **18.** A seed is covered with sap.

_____ **19.** A wooly mammoth freezes in a snowstorm.

_____ **20.** An imprint of fish bones is seen in a rock.

The Ages of Rocks and Fossils

Directions Compare and contrast the two terms below. Explain how they are alike and how they are different.

relative dating—absolute dating

1. How are they alike? _____

_____

_____

2. How are they different? _____

_____

_____

Directions Answer the questions.

3. Give an example of an index fossil and tell how scientists might use such a find.

_____

_____

4. What is the principle of superposition? _____

_____

5. What is the principle of crosscutting relationships? _____

_____

_____

6. How does the half-life of a radioactive element help determine the age of a rock or fossil?

_____

_____

Directions Identify each term below with a method of dating rocks. On the line, write *R* for relative dating or *A* for absolute dating.

7. carbon-14 _____

8. radioactive element _____

9. half-life _____

10. determining actual age _____

11. comparing layers _____

12. crosscutting _____

13. uranium-238 _____

14. index fossil _____

15. superposition _____

Eras in the Geologic Time Scale: Terms Review

Directions Match each term with its description. Write the letter of the correct description on the line.

_____ **1.** principle of superposition

_____ **2.** Paleozoic Era

_____ **3.** geologic time scale

_____ **4.** fossil

_____ **5.** radioactive element

_____ **6.** index fossil

_____ **7.** principle of crosscutting relationships

_____ **8.** petrification

_____ **9.** half-life

_____ **10.** Mesozoic Era

A era marked by trilobites and other sea life

B youngest feature cuts across other rock layers

C fossil that provides clues to the age of a rock

D element that decays to form another element

E outline of the earth's history

F dinosaur era

G oldest rock layer is on the bottom

H minerals replace a buried organism

I preserved remains of an organism

J length of time for half of an element's atoms to decay

Directions 11–18. In each box below, write the numbers 1 to 4 on the lines to show the correct order in geologic history.

_____ Paleozoic Era	_____ Swamps form; coal begins to develop.
_____ Cenozoic Era	_____ The earth's crust and mantle form.
_____ Precambrian Era	_____ The Rocky Mountains form.
_____ Mesozoic Era	_____ The Great Lakes form after the last ice age.

Directions Contrast each pair of terms. Explain how the terms in each pair are different.

19. absolute dating—relative dating _____

_____

_____

20. cast—mold _____

_____

_____

Sources of Fresh Water

Directions Match each term with its description. Write the letter of the correct description on the line.

_____ **1.** divide

_____ **2.** drainage basin

_____ **3.** geyser

_____ **4.** porous

_____ **5.** reservoir

_____ **6.** sinkhole

_____ **7.** spring

_____ **8.** tributary

_____ **9.** water table

A forms when the roof of a cave collapses

B top of the groundwater layer

C river that joins another river

D made by constructing a dam across a river

E hot groundwater and steam shooting into the air

F land area drained by a river and its tributaries

G having many spaces for water and air to flow

H separates two drainage basins

I groundwater flowing naturally out of the ground

Directions Write an answer to each question.

10. How does the sun power the water cycle? _____

_____

11. Where does most runoff eventually end up? _____

_____

12. What two things can happen to precipitation that doesn't sink into the ground?

_____

_____

_____

13. What percent of the earth's water is fresh water? _____

14. How do lakes gain and lose water? _____

_____

_____

15. What are three purposes of reservoirs? _____

_____

_____

_____

Oceans: Terms Review

Directions Write the term from the Word Bank that best completes each sentence.

Word Bank

benthos	divide	mid-ocean ridge	runoff	thermocline
continental shelf	drainage basin	nekton	salinity	trench
continental slope	geysers	porous	seamount	tributary
currents	groundwater	reservoir	sinkhole	water cycle
				water table

1. Precipitation that sinks into the ground becomes _____.

2. Precipitation that does not sink into the ground or evaporate becomes _____.

3. Water moving between the atmosphere and the earth's surface is the _____.

4. A river that joins another river is a _____.

5. When the roof of a cave collapses, a _____ forms.

6. The top of the groundwater layer is the _____.

7. Water can sink into the ground because the soil is _____.

8. The land area in which runoff drains into a large river is a _____.

9. An artificial lake made by building a dam is a _____.

10. A ridge that separates drainage basins is a _____.

11. The saltiness of water is _____.

12. A deep valley in the ocean floor is a _____.

13. A mountain chain on the ocean floor is a _____.

14. The temperature drops sharply in the _____.

15. The part of a continent that extends underwater is the _____.

16. A _____ dips from a continental shelf down to the ocean floor.

17. An underwater mountain that is often a volcano is a _____.

18. Ocean life includes plankton, _____, and _____.

19. Winds cause up-and-down waves as well as flowing ocean streams called _____.

20. Groundwater flows out of springs and blasts out of _____.

Gases in the Atmosphere

Directions 1–10. Put the steps of each cycle in the correct order. Write the numbers 1 to 6 on the lines. (1 is already marked for you.)

The Oxygen-Carbon Dioxide Cycle

_____ They release carbon dioxide into the atmosphere.

__1__ Animals and people breathe in air.

_____ Plants release oxygen into the air.

_____ Plants take in the carbon dioxide through their leaves.

_____ Their bodies use oxygen to change food into energy.

_____ Plants use carbon dioxide to make sugar.

The Nitrogen Cycle

_____ Animals and people take in nitrogen when they eat plants or plant-eating animals.

_____ Bacteria in the soil break down these wastes.

__1__ Bacteria in the soil change nitrogen gas into chemical compounds.

_____ Nitrogen is returned to the soil as animal waste and as dead plants and animals.

_____ Bacteria release nitrogen into the air and into the soil.

_____ Plants take in these nitrogen-containing compounds through their roots.

Directions Answer the questions.

11. What is the atmosphere? _____

_____

12. What percent of the atmosphere is oxygen gas? _____

13. What percent of the atmosphere is nitrogen gas? _____

14. Compare how plants take in nitrogen with how they take in carbon dioxide.

_____

_____

15. Name the four layers of the atmosphere.

_____

_____

Clouds

Directions Write the term from the Word Bank that best completes each sentence. Then find and circle each term in the puzzle.

1. A(n) _____ is a mass of tiny water droplets.

2. The height above the earth's surface is _____.

3. Some clouds form when air is forced up a(n) _____.

4. _____ is a cloud that forms near the ground.

5. There are _____ main types of clouds.

6. Clouds are grouped according to their _____ and altitude.

7. Fluffy _____ clouds are found between 2,000 and 7,000 meters.

8. High, thin, wispy clouds are called _____ clouds.

9. Heat from the sun causes water to _____, or change into gas.

10. When air cools, water vapor in it may _____, or change into liquid.

11. Air contains a gas called water _____.

12. Cirrus and cumulus clouds are often seen in _____ weather.

13. Low, flat clouds that often bring rain are _____ clouds.

14. Fog usually forms in early morning in low areas or over warm _____.

15. Cirrus clouds are made of _____ instead of water droplets.

Word Bank

altitude
cirrus
cloud
condense
cumulus
evaporate
fair
fog
ice crystals
mountain
shape
stratus
three
vapor
water

```
R R O A V F B A N T V A P O R
P B B F L P Z D G N F Z E Z L
C L V E O L D R R M S S E T J
S U A L T I T U D E U T K H E
E T M T H R E E O R U D E R C
S O R U F A I R R Z F M E O L
R N X A L D A I T K O N V T O
C H I L T U C T T N I I A A U
O W O V A U S R P A Y H P A D
N A F F W S S I T P P I O D W
D T M O L J T N W T E A R E E
E E N G E J U B R F P Y A F L
N R N T P O F W R R A U T C U
S Y W X M E C E G T H W E A T
E U G O I C E C R Y S T A L S
```

Wind Patterns: Terms Review

Directions Read the clues to complete the puzzle.

Across

1. moisture falling to the earth

5. water ___: water in a gas phase

6. ___ wind: strong wind just north or south of the equator

8. ___sphere: coldest layer of the atmosphere

9. atmosphere layer that includes ozone

12. cloud near the ground

13. thin, wispy type of cloud

15. polar ___: wind near a pole that brings cold, stormy weather

16. low, flat cloud type

17. prevailing ___: wind blowing from the west

18. wind ___: pattern of wind movement around the earth

Down

2. section of the atmosphere with electrically charged particles

3. bottom layer of the atmosphere

4. wind ___: cycle of air flow

6. outermost layer of the atmosphere

7. to change from a liquid to a gas

10. layer of gases around the earth

11. puffy, white cloud type

13. to change from a gas to a liquid

14. height above the earth's surface

Weather Conditions and Measurements

Directions In the table, write the name of the instrument next to the weather condition it measures.

Name of Instrument	What It Measures
1.	air temperature
2.	air pressure
3.	relative humidity
4.	wind speed
5.	wind direction
6.	amount of rain

Directions Answer the questions.

7. What is weather? _____

_____

8. How are a Fahrenheit thermometer and a Celsius thermometer different?

_____

_____

9. How does an aneroid barometer work? _____

_____

10. What is relative humidity? _____

_____

_____

11. If the front end of a wind vane is pointing west and the back end is pointing east,

which way is the wind blowing? _____

12. What are three ways to measure precipitation? _____

_____

13. A wind is blowing from west to east. Is it a west wind or an east wind? _____

14. The barometric pressure rises from 74 centimeters to 76 centimeters. What kind of

weather may be coming? _____

15. Water freezes and ice melts at 32°F. What is this temperature in Celsius? _____

Weather Patterns and Predictions

Directions Match each term with its description. Write the letter of the correct description on the line.

_____ **1.** cold front

_____ **2.** low

_____ **3.** warm front

_____ **4.** equator

_____ **5.** front

_____ **6.** hurricane

_____ **7.** isobar

_____ **8.** air mass

_____ **9.** thunderhead

_____ **10.** high

_____ **11.** tornado

A section of air having same temperature and humidity

B severe tropical storm with high winds revolving around an eye

C area of high pressure

D powerful wind storm with a funnel-shaped cloud

E line connecting areas of equal air pressure

F near here hurricanes form in the ocean

G cold air mass pushing out and under warm air mass

H warm air mass gliding up and over cooler air mass

I area of low pressure

J boundary line between two air masses

K large, dark cumulus clouds that produce lightning and thunder

Directions Label each diagram with one of these terms: *low* or *high*. On the lines below each diagram, describe the weather conditions that are represented. Consider temperature, precipitation, wind, sky conditions, and air pressure.

12. _____

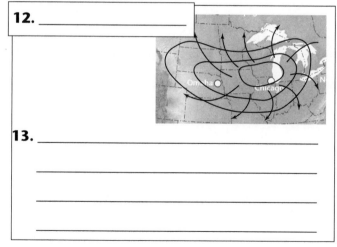

13. _____

_____

_____

_____

14. _____

15. _____

_____

_____

_____

World Climates: Terms Review

Directions Write the answer to the question in each box.

What are the three major climate zones from coldest (1) to warmest (3)? 1. _____ 2. _____ 3. _____	What are three factors that affect climate? 4. _____ 5. _____ 6. _____

Directions Match each term with its definition. Write the letter of the correct definition on the line.

_____ **7.** relative humidity

_____ **8.** hurricane

_____ **9.** tornado

_____ **10.** front

_____ **11.** isobar

_____ **12.** high

_____ **13.** climate

_____ **14.** air pressure

_____ **15.** weather

_____ **16.** low

_____ **17.** air mass

A state of the atmosphere at a given time and place

B amount of water vapor in air compared to the maximum amount of water vapor air can hold

C section of air with the same temperature and humidity

D line on a weather map connecting areas of equal pressure

E tropical storm with high winds revolving around an eye

F powerful wind storm with whirling, funnel-shaped cloud and very low pressure

G cold area of high air pressure

H warm area of low air pressure

I moving boundary line between two air masses

J force of air against a unit of area

K average weather pattern of a region over a long time

Directions Write the weather condition that each instrument measures.

18. anemometer _____

19. psychrometer _____

20. barometer _____

The Solar System

Directions When you compare and contrast things, you tell how they are alike and different. Compare and contrast each pair of terms.

star—planet

1. Alike _____

2. Different _____

planet—moon

3. Alike _____

4. Different _____

moon—star

5. Alike _____

6. Different _____

planet—sun

7. Alike _____

8. Different _____

Directions Write the term from the Word Bank that best completes each sentence.

Word Bank			
chromosphere	helium	nuclear reactions	three
cooler	mass	star	

9. The sun is a _____ because it makes its own energy and light.

10. The sun is made mostly of _____ and hydrogen.

11. The sun's high temperature is caused by _____ inside the sun.

12. The sun's atmosphere has _____ layers.

13. The middle layer of the sun's atmosphere is called the _____.

14. Because sunspots give off less energy, they are _____ than the rest of the sun.

15. The sun contains 99 percent of the _____ in the entire solar system.

The Inner Planets

Directions Look at the diagram. Then write the names of the four inner planets as headings in the chart below. Fill in the rest of the chart.

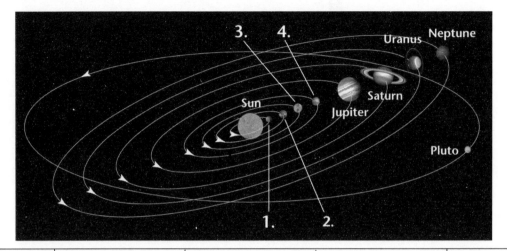

Planet Features	1.	2.	3.	4.
length of rotation	59 Earth days	5.	24 hours	6.
direction of rotation	west to east	7.	8.	west to east
temperature	9.	460°C	10.	colder than Earth
atmosphere	almost none	11.	12.	thinner atmosphere than Earth
surface	13.	plains, highlands, craters	liquid water, life	iron in rocks and soil
number of moons	14.	none	1	15.

The Outer Planets

Directions Look at the diagram. Then write the names of the five outer planets on the lines below.

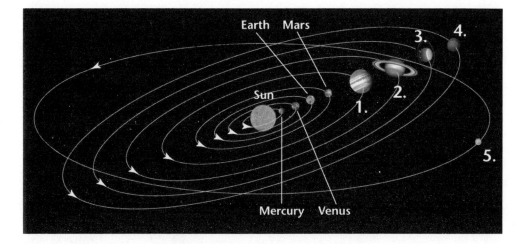

1. _____

2. _____

3. _____

4. _____

5. _____

Directions Write the answer to each question.

6. Which is the only outer planet that does not have a thick atmosphere? _____

7. Which planet is named after the Roman god of the sea? _____

8. Which planet is the largest? _____

9. Which planet rotates on its side? _____

10. Which is the second largest planet in the solar system? _____

11. Which planet has a moon called Charon? _____

12. Which planet takes 84 years to orbit the sun? _____

13. Which planet has a windstorm that has lasted at least 300 years? _____

14. Which planet has a feature called the Great Dark Spot? _____

15. Which planet has a moon called Titan? _____

Other Objects in the Solar System: Terms Review

Directions Match each clue with a term. Write the letter of the correct term on the line.

_____	**1.** fastest-moving planet	**A**	asteroid
_____	**2.** object that makes its own light	**B**	asteroid belt
_____	**3.** planet named for the Roman god of war	**C**	atmosphere
_____	**4.** envelope of gas surrounding an object in space	**D**	comet
_____	**5.** planet that rotates in the opposite direction from the others	**E**	Earth
_____	**6.** cooler, darker area on the sun's surface	**F**	greenhouse effect
_____	**7.** region between Mars and Jupiter where most asteroids are found	**G**	Jupiter
_____	**8.** planet known for its rings	**H**	Mars
_____	**9.** asteroid that enters Earth's atmosphere	**I**	Mercury
_____	**10.** ball of ice, rock, frozen gases, and dust	**J**	meteor
_____	**11.** planet that rotates on its side	**K**	meteorite
_____	**12.** asteroid that hits the surface of a planet or moon	**L**	moon
_____	**13.** large object in space that orbits a star	**M**	Neptune
_____	**14.** object, smaller than a planet, that orbits a star	**N**	planet
_____	**15.** planet that is third from the sun	**O**	Saturn
_____	**16.** star and all of the objects that revolve around it	**P**	solar system
_____	**17.** warming of the atmosphere because of trapped heat energy from the sun	**Q**	star
_____	**18.** largest planet	**R**	sunspot
_____	**19.** satellite that orbits a planet	**S**	Uranus
_____	**20.** greenish-blue planet with the Great Dark Spot	**T**	Venus

Unit 3

Plant and Animal Cells

Directions A Venn diagram shows how two things are alike and different. The Venn diagram below shows which features animal cells and plant cells have in common and which ones they do not. Complete the Venn diagram. On the left side of the diagram, write the cell features that only animal cells have. On the right side of the diagram, write the cell features that only plant cells have. In the center of the diagram, write the cell features that both have.

cell membranes	DNA	mitochondria
cell walls	endoplasmic reticulum	nucleus
chloroplasts	Golgi bodies	ribosomes
cytoplasm	lysosomes	vacuoles

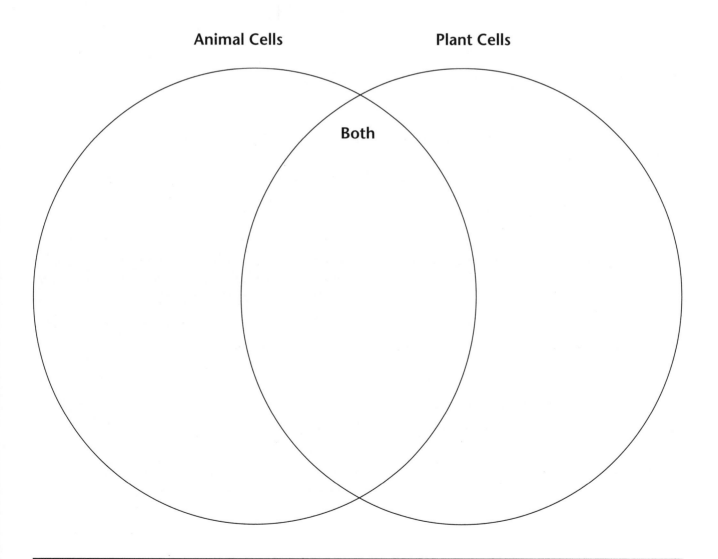

Animal Cells   **Plant Cells**

Both

Chemicals for Life

Directions The following chart shows the chemicals that are important for life.
Complete the chart.

Chemical	Why Is It Important?	Where Is It Found?
1. Water		
2. Carbohydrates		
3. Fats		
4. Proteins		
5. Minerals		
6. Vitamins		

Directions Write your answers on the lines.

7. Use a reference book to find three important vitamins for life. Name some foods they are found in.

_____

_____

8. Use a reference book to find three important minerals for life. Name some foods they are found in.

_____

_____

9. Define amino acids. Tell how they enable proteins to do a wide range of jobs.

_____

_____

10. Compare the role of carbohydrates in plants and in animals.

_____

_____

Basic Life Activities

Directions Complete the crossword puzzle.

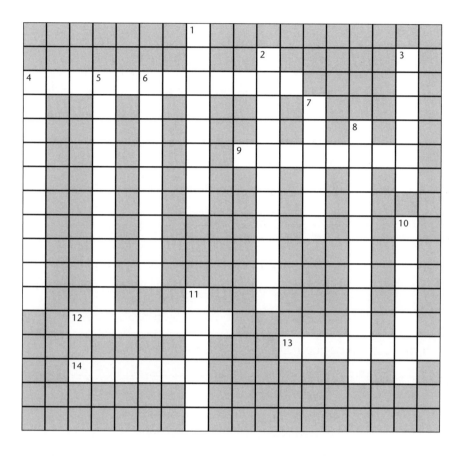

Across

4. process by which living things produce offspring

9. the act of moving

12. living things that eat food and, in most cases, can move freely

13. light, sound, chemicals, and touch that are sensed

14. used to release stored energy during respiration

Down

1. a living thing that reproduces by dividing in two

2. ability of living things to maintain their internal conditions

3. process through which living things reach adult size

4. changing something as a result of a signal

5. process by which living things release energy from food

6. process by which living things break down food

7. used by cells to do work

8. the changes that occur as living things grow

10. one stage in a frog's development

11. living things that make their own food

Vocabulary Review

Directions: Match the terms in Column A with the descriptions in Column B.
Write the letter of the correct answer on the line.

Column A

_____ **1.** microscope

_____ **2.** fungus

_____ **3.** cell

_____ **4.** mineral

_____ **5.** euglena

_____ **6.** bacteria

_____ **7.** vacuole

_____ **8.** lysosome

_____ **9.** photosynthesis

Column B

A food-making process in plants

B living things made of only one cell without organelles

C an instrument that uses light to magnify things

D an organism, such as a mushroom, that decomposes material for food

E a natural substance needed for bodily functions

F the basic unit of life

G stores food, water, or waste

H breaks down substances in animal cells

I a protozoan

Directions: Write the term that is described. Use the words in the Word Bank.

Word Bank		
cell membrane	endoplasmic reticulum	mitochondrion
chloroplast	homeostasis	nucleus

10. control center of the cell _____

11. system of tubes that transports proteins _____

12. thin layer surrounding a cell _____

13. captures light energy from the sun _____

14. uses oxygen to break down food for energy _____

15. the ability of an organism to maintain its internal condition _____

The Classification of Animals

Directions Fill in the missing levels of classification.
Then write levels that are used to show scientific name.

kingdom

1. _____

2. _____

order

family

3. _____

4. _____

5. Scientific name = _____ + _____

Directions Write the word or words needed to complete each sentence.

6. Biologists use a system to classify organisms based on their _____.

7. The highest level in the classification system is _____.

8. The lowest level in the classification system is _____.

9. As you move from an animal's class to its order, it becomes part of a _____
group that is _____ closely related.

10. A scientific name belongs to _____ species.

Directions Answer each question with a phrase or sentence.

11. What does the species level represent?

_____

12. Which animals are more closely related, those in the same order or the same genus?

_____

13. Why do we use scientific names rather than common names in science?

_____

14. What mistakes have been made in writing this scientific name: felis concolor.

_____

15. Why are we unable to say how many kinds of animals there are in the world?

_____

Distinguishing Vertebrates

Directions Name the three characteristics that set vertebrates apart
from other animals.

1. _____

2. _____

3. _____

Directions Complete the table by writing the letter of the correct description for
each group of vertebrates.

Descriptions

  A Have dry, scaly skin. Lay eggs with a soft shell.

  B Have gills, scales, and a skeleton made of cartilage.

  C Have hair and mammary glands.

  D Have gills, scales, and a skeleton made of bone.

  E Have thin, moist skin. As adults, breathe with lungs or through their skin.

  F Have gills and a skeleton made of cartilage. Do not have scales or jaws.

  G Have feathers, hollow bones, and a horny beak. Lay eggs with a hard shell.

Features of Vertebrate Groups

Group	Description	Approximate Number of Species
4. Bony fishes		23,000
5. Sharks, rays, and skates		900
6. Lampreys and hagfishes		90
7. Amphibians		5,000
8. Reptiles		7,000
9. Birds		9,000
10. Mammals		4,300

Invertebrates

Directions: Use terms from the Word Bank to name each kind of invertebrate.

arthropods	echinoderms	mollusks	segmented worms
cnidarians	flatworms	roundworms	sponges

_____ **1.** simplest animals, two layers of tissues, live in water, 10,000 species

_____ **2.** segmented with jointed legs, molt external skeletons, largest group of invertebrates, spider is example

_____ **3.** divided into head, body, and foot; may or may not have shells, 112,000 species; clam is example

_____ **4.** radial symmetry, live in water, 10,000 species, jellyfish is example

_____ **5.** body divided into sections, live in water or soil, 15,000 species, leech is example

_____ **6.** flat and thin, bilateral symmetry, mostly parasites, 20,000 species, tapeworm is example

_____ **7.** long, round bodies; bilateral symmetry; 80,000 species; hookworm is example

_____ **8.** radial symmetry, tube feet, live in the ocean, 7,000 species, sea star is example

Directions: Match each term in Column A with its description in Column B. Write the correct letter on the line.

Column A	Column B
_____ **9.** invertebrate	**A** shedding of the external skeleton
_____ **10.** radial symmetry	**B** arrangement of body parts similar to spokes of a wheel
_____ **11.** tentacle	**C** change of form during development
_____ **12.** bilateral symmetry	**D** animal without a backbone
_____ **13.** molting	**E** structures that echinoderms use to move
_____ **14.** tube feet	**F** body plan showing left and right halves
_____ **15.** metamorphosis	**G** armlike part used for capturing prey

Animals Feeding

Directions Compare and contrast each pair below. Tell how they are alike and how they are different.

1. filter feeders—fluid feeders

   A How they are alike _____

   _____

   B How they are different _____

   _____

2. herbivore—carnivore

   A How they are alike _____

   _____

   B How they are different _____

   _____

3. gastrovascular cavity—digestive tract

   A How they are alike _____

   _____

   B How they are different _____

   _____

Directions Write the word or words needed to complete each sentence.

4. Filter feeders must live in the _____ and have some way to
   _____ food out of the water.

5. Fluid feeders such as aphids and bees have _____ mouthparts.

Animal Respiratory and Circulatory Systems

Directions Write the word or words needed to complete each sentence.

1. Mammals have a heart with _____ chambers.

2. The _____ receive blood returning to the heart.

3. The _____ pump blood out of the heart.

4. Blood returning to the heart contains _____ to be eliminated.

Directions Label the diagram. Begin with the left atrium. Label the parts of the circulatory system.

10. _____

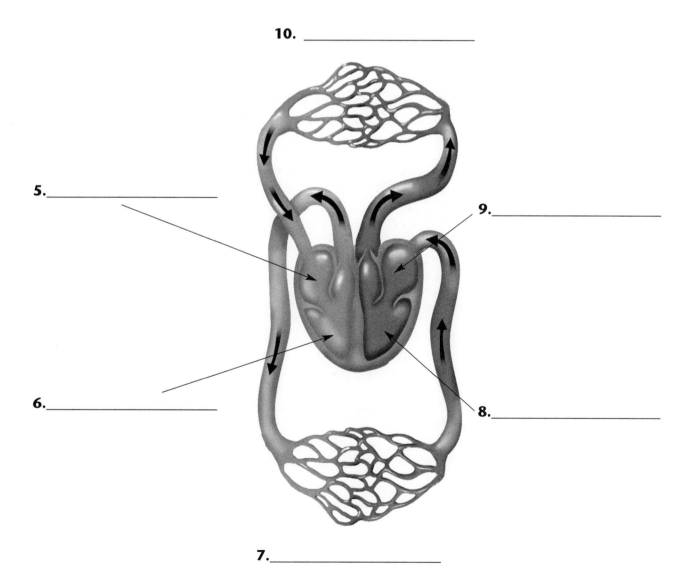

5. _____

9. _____

6. _____

8. _____

7. _____

Vocabulary Review

Directions Match each term with its description. Write the correct letter on the line.

Column A

_____ **1.** genus

_____ **2.** tentacle

_____ **3.** cold-blooded

_____ **4.** metamorphosis

_____ **5.** cartilage

_____ **6.** warm-blooded

_____ **7.** gill

_____ **8.** gestation time

_____ **9.** molting

_____ **10.** tube foot

_____ **11.** vertebra

_____ **12.** phylum

_____ **13.** species

_____ **14.** asexual reproduction

_____ **15.** sexual reproduction

Column B

A a material in vertebrate skeletons, softer than bone

B breathing structure for vertebrates that live in water

C small tube used by echinoderms for moving

D shedding of external skeleton, characteristic of arthropods

E having a body temperature that changes with surrounding temperatures

F changes in form during development

G having a body temperature that stays the same

H reproduction involving two parents and sex cells

I the sixth classification level of biology, contains separate species

J arm-like body part of invertebrates, used to catch prey

K a group of organisms that can breed with each other to produce offspring like themselves

L subdivision of a kingdom with the second largest group of organisms

M period of time from fertilization to birth

N one of the bones or blocks of cartilage that make up a backbone

O reproduction involving one parent and no egg or sperm

Classifying Plants

Directions Use the clue to complete the word or words below it. Hint: Vowels are missing in the answer blocks.

Two scientists who worked to classify plants

1. | | r | | s | t | | t | l | | |

2. | L | | n | n | | | | s |

Two groups in scientific names of plants

3. | g | | n | | s |

4. | s | p | | c | | | s |

Genus and species of the red maple

5. | | c | | r |

6. | r | | b | r | | m |

Plant tissue containing tubes; also, an example in a leaf

7. | v | | s | c | | l | | r |

8. | v | | | n |

Well-developed parts in vascular plants

9 . | s | t | | m | s |

10. | l | | | v | | s |

11. | r | | | t | s |

Plants that do not have tubelike cells

12. | n | | n | v | | s | c | | l | | r |

What plants without tubelike cells must always have nearby

13. | m | | | s | t | | r | |

Cluster of fern's reproductive cells, the reproductive cells

14. | s | | r | |

15. | s | p | | r | | s |

The Vascular System in Plants

Directions Complete the chart. Identify the plant parts and their functions.
Then answer the question.

Plant Structure	Part	Functions
Root	root tip	**3.**
	vascular tissue	**4.**
	1. xylem	**5.**
	2.	**6.**

Stem	**7.**	**10.**
	8.	**11.**
	9.	**12.**

Leaf	**13.**	**16.**
	14.	**17.**
	15.	**18.**
		19.

20. In what ways are the roots and stems of a plant alike and different?

_____

_____

_____

How Plants Make Food

Directions Complete the crossword puzzle.

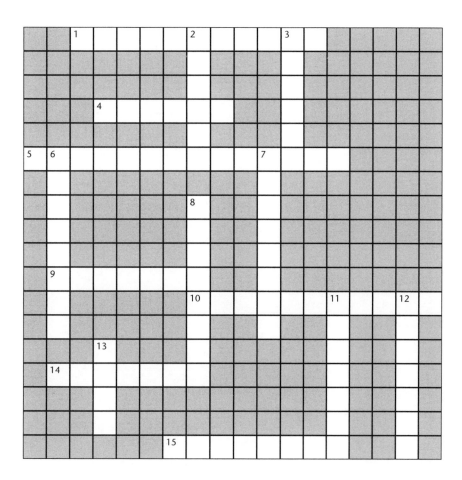

Across

1. Green pigment in plants that absorbs light energy

4. Living things need _____.

5. Process in which a plant makes food

9. Simple sugar

10. Organelle where photosynthesis occurs

14. Plants need carbon _____ to make food.

15. Source of energy for photosynthesis

Down

2. A product of photosynthesis

3. Plant parts that contain many chloroplasts

6. What H stands for in H_2O

7. $6CO_2 + 6H_2O +$ light energy $\rightarrow C_6H_{12}O_6 + 6O_2$ is the _____ for photosynthesis.

8. One product of photosynthesis is one _____ of sugar.

11. A chemical that absorbs certain types of light

12. Oxygen leaves a plant through _____.

13. Photosynthesis provides _____ for plants and people.

Vocabulary Review

Directions Match the terms in Column A with the descriptions in Column B.
Write the letter of each correct answer on the line.

Column A

_____ **1.** angiosperm

_____ **2.** phloem

_____ **3.** gymnosperm

_____ **4.** moss

_____ **5.** ovary

_____ **6.** xylem

_____ **7.** stigma

_____ **8.** sori

_____ **9.** petiole

_____ **10.** stamen

_____ **11.** rhizome

_____ **12.** pollen

_____ **13.** rhizoid

_____ **14.** pigment

_____ **15.** germinate

Column B

A stalk that attaches a leaf to a stem

B male organ of reproduction in a flower

C vascular tissue in plant that carries food throughout plant

D tiny grains containing sperm

E plant part with shoots aboveground and roots belowground

F chemical that absorbs certain kinds of light

G vascular tissue that carries water and minerals from roots to stems and leaves

H nonvascular plant

I rootlike thread of a moss plant

J flowering plant

K nonflowering seed plant

L start to grow into a new plant

M lower part of the pistil that contains eggs

N clusters of spores on fern leaves

O upper part of the pistil, on the tip of the style

Ecology Crossword

Directions Fill in the blank or write the term to complete the puzzle.

Across

1. number of an organism living in a set area
3. that part of earth where organisms can live
5. various populations living in one area
6. living factors in an environment
7. used by organisms to live; water, air, sunlight are examples
8. _____ species have few members left.
13. All organisms ___ with living and nonliving things in their environment.
14. An _____ is all the interactions among the populations of a community and its nonliving parts.
15. process by which a community changes over time

Down

1. something harmful to organisms that is added to an environment
2. ___ rain contains sulfuric or nitric acid.
4. resources Earth cannot replace, such as minerals
6. ecosystem covering large area, for example, an ocean or a desert
9. place an organism lives
10. fuel formed long ago from remains of organisms
11. A ___ community is stable and contains many types of organisms.
12. study of interactions among living and nonliving parts of an environment

Food Chains and Food Webs

Directions Use the terms to complete the paragraph.

decomposers	food webs	second-order consumers
first-order consumers	large	small
food chain	photosynthesis	third-order consumers

Every **1.** _____ begins with a producer. Most producers

make their food by **2.** _____. Producers are eaten by

3. _____. Animals that eat these plant-eaters are called

4. _____. They are eaten by **5.** _____.

The food chain begins with a **6.** _____ number of

producers. It ends with a **7.** _____ number of last-order

consumers. Because few consumers eat only one type of food, food

chains are linked in **8.** _____. Food chains do not end

because **9.** _____ feed on dead animals.

Directions Use the terms to complete the paragraph.

consumers	energy	pyramid of numbers
decreases	food chain	sugars

Plants use **10.** _____ from the Sun to make food. They use light

energy to make **11.** _____ and other molecules. Organisms that eat

other organisms because they cannot make their own food are **12.** _____.

As organisms eat each other, energy moves through the **13.** _____.

The amount of energy available **14.** _____ at each higher level of the

food chain. The **15.** _____ shows the sizes of the populations at

different levels of the food chain.

Energy Flow in an Ecosystem

Directions Finish each explanation for the flow of energy in a food chain using the words in the box. You'll use some words more than once.

1. Unlimited energy comes from the _____

2. Energy used for _____

3. Energy lost as _____

4. Energy stored in _____

5. Energy used for _____

6. Energy lost as _____

7. Energy stored in _____

body tissues
heat
life activities
plant tissues
sun

Directions Answer each question.

8. Who receives the energy stored in first-order consumers?

   _____

9. To which organisms is the most energy available? Why?

   _____

10. To which organisms is the least energy available? Why?

    _____

11. Why is a pyramid shape used to show amounts of energy available at each level of a food chain?

    _____

12. In the energy pyramid featured on page 510, which organism has the least amount of energy available?

    _____

13. Why is there a much bigger population of grasshoppers than of foxes?

    _____

14. Why is the sun so important to the food chain?

    _____

15. How does energy flow in an ecosystem? Use the words *producers*, *sun*, and *consumers* in your answer.

    _____

Vocabulary Review

Directions Match each term in Column A with its meaning in Column B.
Write the correct letter on the line.

Column A

_____ **1.** energy pyramid

_____ **2.** threatened

_____ **3.** succession

_____ **4.** community

_____ **5.** fossil fuels

_____ **6.** food web

_____ **7.** consumer

_____ **8.** carrying capacity

_____ **9.** renewable resource

_____ **10.** groundwater

Column B

A a process through which a community changes over time

B the water that sinks beneath the earth's surface

C fewer members of a species exist now than before

D natural resource that nature replaces

E a set of populations living in the same area

F number of individuals an environment can support

G formed long ago from the remains of organisms

H diagram comparing the amounts of energy available to different levels of the food chain

I linked food chains in a community through which energy moves

J an organism that feeds on other organisms; unable to make its own food

Directions Unscramble the word or words in parentheses to complete each sentence below.

11. A poison gas mixes with rain to form _____, which harms organisms. (daic anri)

12. Living things are biotic, and nonliving things are _____. (atiiboc)

13. An endangered animal population could become _____ if all its members die off. (ttexnic)

14. Liquid water _____ from water vapor. (nodnecses)

15. Fossil fuels are examples of _____ resources that cannot be replaced. (nelannerobew)

Chromosomes

Directions Complete the chart. Use it to show how each pair of items is alike and different.

	Similarities	Differences
Meiosis/Mitosis	**1.**	**2.**
XX zygote/XY zygote	**3.**	**4.**
Human sex cells/ Human body cells	**5.**	**6.**
Human egg cells/ Human sperm cells	**7.**	**8.**
Heredity/Environment	**9.**	**10.**

Directions Define each term.

11. gene

_____

12. chromosome

_____

13. mutation

_____

14. base

_____

15. adaptation

_____

Vocabulary Review

Directions Match each term with its description. Write the correct letter on the line.

Column A	Column B
_____ **1.** vestigial structure	**A** testable explanation of a question or problem
_____ **2.** adaptation	**B** the passing of traits from parents to offspring
_____ **3.** heredity	**C** rod-shaped structure that contains DNA and is in the cell's nucleus
_____ **4.** homologous structure	**D** a useless body part in an organism that may have been useful to its ancestors
_____ **5.** natural selection	
_____ **6.** diversity	**E** theory that recent species are changed descendants of earlier species
_____ **7.** descent with modification	**F** the changes in a population over time
_____ **8.** replicate	**G** to make a copy of
_____ **9.** meiosis	**H** molecule in DNA that is used to code information
_____ **10.** adaptive advantage	**I** process by which organisms best suited to the environment survive and pass their genes on
_____ **11.** environment	**J** process that results in two cells identical to the parent cell
_____ **12.** hypothesis	
_____ **13.** scientific theory	**K** a change that makes an organism better able to survive in its environment
_____ **14.** genetics	**L** generally accepted and well-tested scientific explanation
_____ **15.** chromosome	**M** an organism's surroundings
_____ **16.** evolution	**N** body part that is similar in related organisms
_____ **17.** mutation	**O** section of DNA that carries a trait
_____ **18.** mitosis	**P** the study of heredity
_____ **19.** gene	**Q** range of differences found in a population
_____ **20.** base	**R** a change in a gene
	S organism's greater chance of survival because of characteristics
	T the process that results in sex cells

Unit 4

The Skeletal and Muscular Systems

Directions Complete the sentences with the correct terms from the Word Bank.

Word Bank			
cardiac muscles	ligaments	skeletal system	trachea
cartilage	muscular system	skull	vertebrae
involuntary muscles	osteoporosis	smooth muscles	voluntary muscles
joints	red marrow	tendons	

1. The human _____ is made up of 206 bones.

2. Before birth, the entire skeleton is made up of _____, a thick, smooth tissue.

3. A person could develop _____ if calcium released by the bones into the bloodstream is not replaced.

4. The 33 _____ of the backbone protect the spinal cord.

5. The _____ protects the brain.

6. Bones come together at _____ where cartilage acts like a cushion.

7. Bones have spongy material called _____ that produces blood cells.

8. Cartilage surrounds the _____, the tube that carries air to the lungs.

9. At joints, _____ connect bones to each other.

10. The _____ works with the skeletal system to produce movement.

11. Bones are connected to muscles by _____.

12. Skeletal muscles, which a person can move at will, are _____.

13. The stomach has _____ that move food through the digestive system.

14. The _____ in the heart contract to pump blood through the body.

15. The smooth muscles and cardiac muscles are _____ that cannot be controlled.

Digestion

Directions Label the parts of the human digestive system.

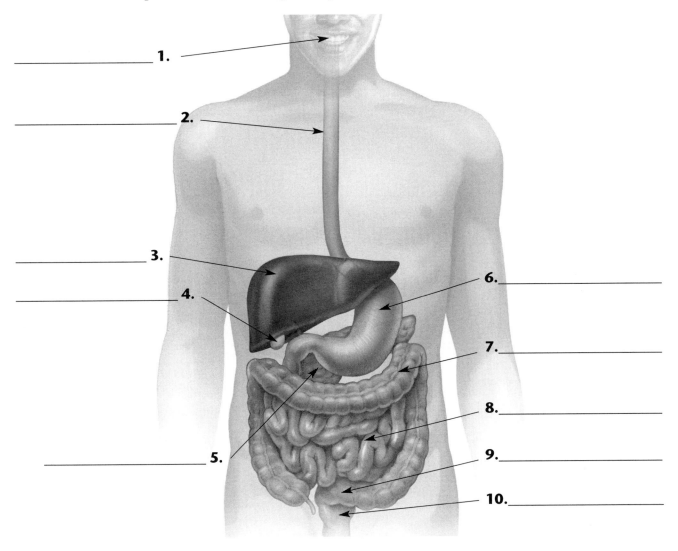

_____ **1.**

_____ **2.**

_____ **3.**

_____ **4.**

_____ **5.**

6. _____

7. _____

8. _____

9. _____

10. _____

Directions Complete the sentences with the correct terms from the diagram.

11. The _____ is a large organ that makes a fluid called bile.

12. Liquid food called chyme enters the _____ from the stomach.

13. The main function of the _____ is to remove water from undigested material.

14. The _____ breaks down food with powerful acids.

15. The _____ is the place where digestion begins.

In Circulation

Directions Find the words from Lesson 3 that best solve the clues.
Then write the letters in the blank spaces running across or down.

Across

1. This tiny blood vessel has a wall only one cell thick.

5. The color of blood

6. A blood vessel that carries blood away from the heart

7. The liquid part of blood is called _____.

9. A blood vessel that carries blood to the heart

10. The blood in arteries is _____ in oxygen.

11. A, B, AB, and O each represent a different blood _____.

12. The heart pumps _____ through the body.

15. The organs that fill blood with oxygen

Down

2. Tiny cell pieces that help blood to clot

3. These cells make up almost half of the blood. (3 words)

4. A vein carrying blood _____ a lung is full of oxygen.

8. A protein in plasma that fights disease

13. Without oxygen, cells _____.

14. Capillaries reach every _____ in the body.

Respiration

Directions Label the parts of the human respiratory system below.

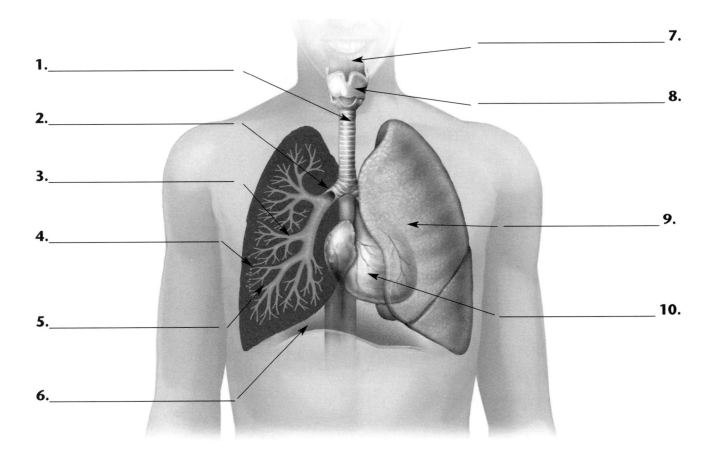

1. _____

2. _____

3. _____

4. _____

5. _____

6. _____

7. _____

8. _____

9. _____

10. _____

Directions Complete the sentences with the correct terms from the diagram.

11. The _____ is a strong muscle that helps you breathe.

12. Air moves from the pharynx through the _____, or voice box.

13. Another name for the _____ is windpipe.

14. The _____ carry air to microscopic air sacs called alveoli.

15. Both air and food share the passageway known as the _____.

Excretion

Directions Answer the questions with a word or phrase.

1. How many layers of skin do you have?   _____

2. Which layer of skin helps keep in heat?   _____

3. What substance do your sweat glands release?   _____

4. What good effect does perspiration have on a hot day?   _____

5. The kidneys are the main organs of what system?   _____

6. How many kidneys does the human body have?   _____

7. What do the kidneys filter in order to collect waste?   _____

8. What tubes carry urine out of the kidneys?   _____

9. Where does urine collect?   _____

10. What tube carries urine out of the body?   _____

Directions Answer each question in one or two complete sentences.

11. How are urine and perspiration alike?

_____

_____

12. Where is the dermis in relation to the epidermis?

_____

_____

13. Why does your body get rid of wastes?

_____

_____

14. What do water, heat, salt, and nitrogen have in common?

_____

_____

15. How is the waste in your body similar to the waste in your home or community?

_____

_____

Vocabulary Review

Directions Match the terms in Column A with its meaning in Column B.
Write the correct letter on the line.

Column A	Column B
_____ **1.** arteries	**A** tube that carries air to the bronchi
_____ **2.** testosterone	**B** branches of the bronchi in the lungs
_____ **3.** excretory system	**C** blood vessels that carry blood away from the heart
_____ **4.** trachea	**D** organ that produces chemicals for the body's use
_____ **5.** estrogen	**E** the digestive organ that stores bile
_____ **6.** gland	**F** male sex hormone
_____ **7.** capillaries	**G** tube through which eggs move from an ovary to the uterus
_____ **8.** urine	**H** blood vessels that carry blood to the heart
_____ **9.** veins	**I** tiny blood vessels that are one cell thick
_____ **10.** gallbladder	**J** the network of bones in the body
_____ **11.** larynx	**K** a series of organs that get rid of cell wastes in the form of urine
_____ **12.** skeletal system	**L** female sex hormone
_____ **13.** bronchioles	**M** gland that produces the fluid in semen
_____ **14.** prostate gland	**N** the voice box
_____ **15.** fallopian tube	**O** liquid waste formed in the kidneys

Directions Write the letter of the word that best completes each sentence.

_____ **16.** The _____ is the layer of skin with blood vessels, nerves, and glands.

    A fatty layer   **B** ligament   **C** epidermis   **D** dermis

_____ **17.** Voice box is another name for the _____.

    A trachea   **B** larynx   **C** pharynx   **D** bronchus

_____ **18.** _____ in red blood cells carries oxygen.

    A Hemoglobin   **B** Antibodies   **C** Plasma   **D** Platelets

_____ **19.** _____ is the movement of food being pushed from the esophagus to the stomach.

    A Peristalsis   **B** Digestion   **C** Ovulation   **D** Chyme

_____ **20.** The _____ connects an embryo to the placenta.

    A uterus   **B** progesterone   **C** umbilical cord   **D** fallopian tube

The Senses of Sight and Hearing

Directions Label the parts of the human eye and ear below. Answer the question about the eye.

Eye

1._____

2._____

3._____

4._____

_____ **5.**

_____ **6.**

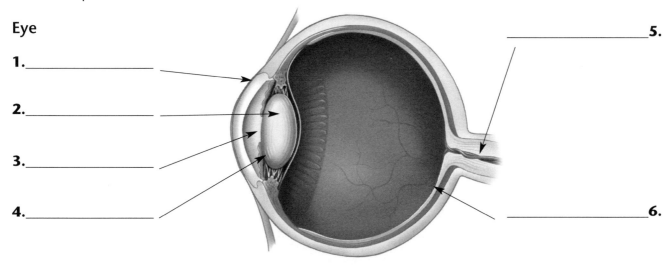

7. When you look at the eye, which feature appears colored? _____

Ear

8._____

9._____

_____ **10.**

_____ **11.**

_____ **12.**

_____ **13.**

_____ **14.**

_____ **15.**

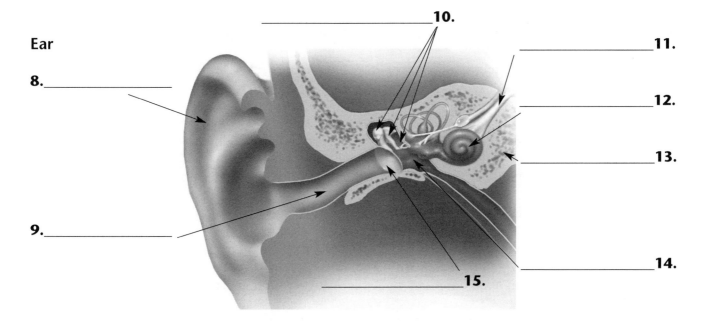

Vocabulary Review

Directions Circle the term in parentheses that best completes each sentence.

1. To move between neurons, impulses must cross small gaps called (synapses, nerves).

2. In the eye, the lens focuses light rays onto the (cornea, retina).

3. Sound waves striking the (eardrum, cochlea) cause it to vibrate.

4. The (cerebellum, cerebrum), which controls what you think, feel, learn, and remember, is the largest part of the brain.

5. The teenage years are called (adolescence, puberty).

6. The (lens, iris) controls the amount of light that enters the eye.

7. The (cornea, pupil) is the black circle in the center of the eye.

8. (Neurons, Receptor cells) in the sense organs receive information about the outside world.

9. Both the (optic nerve and auditory nerve, cochlea and cornea) send impulses to the brain.

10. The (cochlea, eardrum) is a tube in the ear that contains many receptor cells and fluid.

11. The part of the brain that controls balance is the (brain stem, cerebellum).

12. (Adolescence, Puberty) is a period of rapid growth and development during the early teen years.

13. The brain and the spinal cord are connected by the (brain stem, cerebrum).

14. Messages carried from one nerve cell to another are called (neurons, impulses).

15. The body has three kinds of (dentrites, neurons)—sensory, motor, and association.

16. The (backbone, spinal cord) is a thick bunch of nerves that extends from the brain down the back.

17. Impulses are sent from sense organs to the brain by (association neurons, sensory neurons).

18. The sense of taste depends in a large part on the sense of (sight, smell).

19. Insulin and adrenaline are examples of (hormones, glands).

20. Hormones are (chemical messengers, electrical messengers) secreted by glands.